Great Cakes Without Eggs.

(The Hare Krishna Library of Eggless Baking, Part 1)

Akinchana Dasi and Bhagavat Dharma

Bhima Books

Great Cakes Without Eggs.

(The Hare Krishna Library of Eggless Baking, Part 1)

By Akinchana Dasi and Bhagavat Dharma

Published by Bhima Books,
c/o Bhaktivedanta Manor
Letchmore Heath
Watford
WD2 8EP
UK.

Designed and Typeset by Bhagavat Dharma
Cover by Beaver Graphics, Watford, Herts.

Printed by MRM Graphics, Winslow, Bucks.

Line drawings by Chakranadi Dasi, except drawing of Srila Prabhupada by Ananta Shakti Das

Published by Bhima Books, Watford, England, 1993-96.

First edition,	1993	1000 copies
Second revised edition,	1996	3000 copies

ISBN 0-9522-117-2-6

Bhima Books

CONTENTS

THE HARE KRISHNA LIBRARY OF EGGLESS BAKING. ________ *vi*

DEDICATION. ________ *viii*

INTRODUCTION. ________ *x*

MAKING A CAKE FOR KRISHNA. ________ *xii*

- *GOOD BAKING PRACTICE.* ________ *xiii*
- *WHAT WENT WRONG?* ________ *xiv*

CONVENTIONS. ________ *xvi*

"WITH THIS BANANA I THEE WED" - Cakes With Bananas. ________ 1

NO MEAT, FISH, EGGS - OR CHOCOLATE - Cakes With Carob. ________ 15

MAKING LEMON JUICE FOR KRISHNA - Cakes With Citrus Fruits. ________ 32

THE SACRED WATERS OF LETCHMORE HEATH - Cakes With Coconut. ________ 50

GATHERING THE AUTUMN HARVEST - Cakes With Fresh Fruit. ________ 57

GIFTS FOR DIWALI - Light Dried Fruit Cakes. ________ 86

A WALK IN THE AFRICAN NIGHT - Cakes With Nuts. ________ 111

INDIA - LAND OF PLENTY - Moist And Rich Dried Fruit Cakes. ________ 122

THE COSMIC POWER OF GINGER - Cakes With Spices. ________ 138

FOOD FOR LIFE - Cakes Made With Vegetables. ________ 172

APPENDIX - Ingredients Used In This Book. ________ 193

THE HARE KRISHNA LIBRARY OF EGGLESS BAKING.

'Great Cakes Without Eggs' is part one of 'The Hare Krishna Library of Eggless Baking', a series of baking books with ingredients according to the *Vaishnava* tradition. It is also available as a hypertext Winhelp version, from sites on the Internet. The second volume in the Library, 100 Brilliant Biscuits Without Eggs, was published in 1994. Work is in progress on a revised edition of this book, and also a hypertext version.

Our current (April 1996) work in progress is a book of Pies, Tarts and Cheesecakes. We plan to produce books on yeastcakes, breads, savouries and puddings - all without eggs. We are also working on a version of Great Cakes for publication in India, using ingredients available in the sub-continent.

Our future plans are to bring more of the traditional Vaishnava cuisine to the attention of the world. We are researching Vaishnava vegetarian cooking in three areas of India - Bengal, Gujerat and the southern states of Tamil Nadu, Karnataka, Kerala and Andhra Pradesh.

We are interested to work in partnership with Vaishnavas of any tradition, and those interested in spreading the traditions of Vaishnava cooking. Please write and let us discuss how we can work together for our mutual benefit to spread this important and forward-looking tradition.

The hypertext version of 'Great Cakes without Eggs' is available as shareware from all Simtel mirrors on the Internet, in the 'Windows\Food' directory. It is also available on the current Simtel CD-Roms. The most recent version can be obtained from

`ftp://ftp.demon.co.uk/pub/food/eggless/great*.zip,`

`ftp://ftp.idiscover.net/pub/food/eggless/great*.zip`

where * is the latest version.

DEDICATION.

His Divine Grace Srila A.C. Bhaktivedanta Swami Prabhupada.
Founder-Acarya of the International Society for Krishna Consciousness.
Drawing by Ananta Shakti das.

Hinduism has been present in the West since the time of the Conference of Religions in Chicago of 1893. It was not, however, until the arrival of A. C. Bhaktivedanta Swami Prabhupada in New York in 1965, that the tradition of *Vaishnavism* became well-known. *Vaishnavism* stands distinct from the 'All-is-one' philosophy commonly associated with Hinduism, and teaches that there is one God, Krishna, with whom each of us has a personal relationship.

Srila Prabhupada was a visionary, who saw the urgent need for a spiritual revival. He taught a 'Peace Formula', based on reciting the names of God, dancing for the pleasure of God and feasting on sanctified vegetarian foods. He began organic farming projects and opened vegetarian restaurants. He started 'Food for Life' the Hare Krishna free food distribution programme which has fed tens of thousands in Bengal, Philadelphia, Natal, London, Moscow, Sarajevo, Chechnya and throughout the world. He opened temples and lectured on the *Bhagavad Gita* and other scriptures in the *Vaishnava* tradition. He was the first to translate, from Sanskrit into English, the *Srimad Bhagavatam*, an extensive work describing the personality of God.

Srila Prabhupada saw that materialism was polluting the planet and the consciousness of humankind. He was sensitive about the savage exploitation of animals, who he would characterise as 'Our brothers and sisters'. He stressed a delicious and nutritious diet without meat, fish or eggs.

He was an expert cook, philosopher, communicator and guide. He was progressive, compassionate and always enthusiastic to speak about Lord Krishna. He passed from this world in 1977, a harbinger of a spiritual revolution. This publication is dedicated to him, with our gratitude.

INTRODUCTION.

Vegetarianism is now common in the West. A sea-change in eating habits has taken place. Continual health scares and sensitivity to suffering have nurtured this change. To enjoy a good standard of health, nutrition and enjoyment, there is no need to use any ingredient from the meat industry.

We collected and tested these recipes over five years. Our aim was to encourage our friends and fellow devotees in their baking. We later realised that our work could be useful for lacto-vegetarians throughout the world. We are both committed Hare Krishna members, trying to follow the deep and ancient culture of *Vaishnavism.* One of the highest goals of this culture is the protection of cows. *Vaishnava* culture outlines a relationship between humankind and the cow, which is fundamental for the well-being of both.

It is clear to thinking people that today's consumer society has reduced animals to the level of objects. As we publish this second edition, the British government is ready to slaughter millions of cows to 'restore confidence in the beef market', after it's own scientists revealed a connection between the cattle disease BSE. and a human equivalent, Creutzfelt-Jacob disease.

We respect people who follow a Vegan way of life, giving up all contact with animal products. We have included Vegan recipes in each section of this publication. The *Vaishnava* understanding is that milk is essential for a healthy body and mind. The Hare Krishna movement is setting up non-violent farm projects throughout the world. At the British headquarters at Bhaktivedanta Manor, near Watford, the movement has recently quadrupled the acreage available for Britain's first cow protection programme.

This work was first published in 1993, and has sold over 1,000 copies. For this second edition, we have added American cup measures, and incorporated much of the feedback we have got in the last two years. The other major addition is a section on ingredients. We welcome any feedback from readers and users; please write or send e-mail to the addresses below. We will do our best to answer any queries you may have. We particularly welcome your comments and suggestions for improvement.

Akinchana Dasi and Bhagavat Dharma, Bhima Books, c/o Bhaktivedanta Manor, Letchmore Heath, Watford, WD2 8EP, UK.

e-mail; bhagavat.dharma.mg@com.bbt.se

MAKING A CAKE FOR KRISHNA.

Vaishnavism, the philosophy of the Hare Krishna movement has been described as the 'Culture of gratitude.' Gratitude to the Supreme Person, gratitude to those who have made sacrifices on our behalf and gratitude to each other for each and every kindness. Offering food, with a sense of gratitude, to Krishna, is one of the main religious practices of a devotee. In the Bhagavad Gita, Krishna explains what kinds of food he accepts

'If one offers Me with love and devotion a leaf, a flower, fruit or water, I will accept it.' ***Bhagavad Gita 9.26.***

Elsewhere, the Vaishnava scriptures explain that Krishna will accept milk products, vegetables, fruits, nuts and grains. Meat, fish and eggs are rejected. Garlic, onions and stimulating drinks such as those which contain caffeine, are also ruled out, as they agitate the mind. A devotee is careful when shopping to avoid food containing meat products such as gelatine, or rennin.

Offering food to Krishna is an act of meditation. You should make sure the kitchen is clean and put away anything that has touched meat. You should wash your hands and not taste the food during preparation. Keep a special plate solely for making the offering. When the cake or other food is ready, put a small portion on Krishna's plate and place it beside His picture. You can, in your own words, quietly ask the Lord to accept what you have cooked, and recite the Hare Krishna mantra three times.

Hare Krishna, Hare Krishna, Krishna Krishna, Hare Hare,
Hare Rama Hare Rama, Rama Rama, Hare Hare.

After five minutes or so, you can remove the offering from your small altar and take it from Krishna's plate, which you should clean straight away.

The food you have cooked has now become prasadam, or Krishna's mercy. He has purified the food by accepting it, and anyone who takes His prasadam will receive spiritual benefit.

This important Vaishnava function is carried out each day in millions of households , and in temples large and small in India and throughout the world.

GOOD BAKING PRACTICE.

In order to avoid some of the common faults in cake making, it's useful to bear in mind the following points:

Have all the ingredients and utensils in front of you before you start work.

Follow the measures closely for the first time, before you make any modifications.

Always use the size of tin specified. failure to do so will give unpredictable results.

Preheat the oven before you start. Most cakes should be baked in the middle shelf, unless otherwise stated. Placing them in the top or bottom, may lead to problems.

Do not open the oven door and let in cold air before the cake has had time to set. Don't test for readiness until ten minutes before time, and always use a warm knife. Never slam the oven door.

Test light sponge cakes by pressing the surface lightly with a finger. If the cake springs back, it is done. If the finger impression remains, the cake is not ready.

Test rich fruit cakes by listening carefully to them in the oven. If they 'sizzle' or 'hum', they are not yet ready. Look also to see if they have shrunk away from the sides of the tin.

Always leave the cake in the tin for at least ten minutes after removing from the oven. During this time, the cake will 'firm up' and also shrink slightly from the sides. After turning out, the cake should be placed on a wire tray, which allows circulation of air (and drying) underneath. Rich fruit cakes should be allowed to cool completely in the tin.

WHAT WENT WRONG?

Unfortunately, things do go wrong. Some of the common reasons are given below:

THE CAKE IS SUNK IN THE CENTRE:

- Too much raising agent used.
- The butter (or oil) and sugar were beaten for too long.
- Too much liquid or too little flour was used.
- The oven door was opened too early or slammed.
- The cake was taken out of the oven too early.
- The oven was too hot and the cake rose too fast.

THE CAKE IS BADLY CRACKED OR 'PEAKED':

- Too much raising agent used.
- Too much cake mixture for the size of tin.
- The oven was too hot, or the cake was too near the top.
- Butter (oil) and sugar not creamed enough.
- Too little or too much liquid.

THE TEXTURE OF THE CAKE IS MOIST AND HEAVY:

- Too much liquid.
- Too much sugar
- Too little raising agent
- Insufficient creaming of butter (oil) and sugar.
- Oven too cool, or cake placed at the bottom of the oven.

THE FRUIT HAS SUNK TO THE BOTTOM:

- Too much raising agent, cake rose too fast.
- Fruit wet when placed in mixture. Coat fruit in flour first.
- Glacé fruit too syrupy. Syrup should be washed off and fruit dried.
- Too much liquid in mixture.

THE CAKE IS DRY AND CRUMBLY:

- Too much raising agent.
- Too long a cooking time in too cool an oven.
- Oven too hot.
- Mixture too dry.
- Butter (oil) not rubbed in properly.

THE CAKE HAS A HARD CRUST.

- Too much sugar.
- Oven too hot.
- Cake left in the oven too long.
- The sugar used was too coarse.
- Butter (oil) and sugar were not well creamed.

THE CAKE HAS AN UNEVEN TEXTURE.

- Butter (oil) not rubbed in well.
- Insufficient mixing.
- Air pockets caused by not putting all the mixture in the tin at once.

CONVENTIONS

Abbreviations.

Throughout the book, the following abbreviations are used.....

1 tsp. = 1 teaspoon.
1 tbs. = 1 tablespoon.
bicarb. = Bicarbonate of soda.
conc. = Concentrated.

Oven temperatures.

Equivalent temperatures for various ovens are given below.

Centigrade°	Fahrenheit°	Gas Mark	Oven Heat
110	225	¼	Very cool
120	250	½	Cool
140	275	1	Very slow
150	300	2	Slow
160	325	3	Moderately slow
180	350	4	Moderate
190	375	5	Moderately hot
200	400	6	Fairly hot
220	425	7	Hot
230	450	8	Very hot
240	475	9	Extremely hot

Measurements.

The tables on the following page give the measures used throughout this book. For weight and volume, we recommend using one set of measures. There is not exact equivalence. Cup and Pint sizes in the volume chart refer to American sizes. British cups are slightly larger, and hold 10 fl. ozs, or half a pint. We have given American cup sizes, and not British, as most British bakers use scales rather than cup measures. Note that an American pint is 16 fl. ozs, as opposed to 20 for British. The Australian standard cup size is now 250 ml, which is equivalent to the American cup. Slight variations in standard tablespoon sizes between the three systems have been ignored.

Weight

Oz.	Gms
1	25
2	50
3	75
4	100
5	150
6	175
7	200
8	225
9	250
10	275
11	300
12	350
13	375
14	400
15	425
16	450
17	475
18	500

Volume

Tsp.	Tbs.	Ml.	Fl. oz	US Cups	US Pints
¼		1 ¼			
½		2 ½			
1		5			
3	1	15			
6	2	30	1		
	4	60	2		
	5	90	3		
	8	125	4	½	¼
	10	150	5		
		200	7		
		250	8	1	½
		360	12	1 ½	¾
		480	16	2	1
		720	24	3	1 ½
		960	32	4	2

"WITH THIS BANANA I THEE WED"

CAKES WITH BANANAS

Bhaktivedanta Manor is the main British centre of the Hare Krishna movement. Beatle George Harrison donated the building and Srila Prabhupada consecrated the shrine in 1973. The temple is very popular with Hindus from the North London area, particularly around the time of major festivals like *Janmastami* and *Diwali*.

The temple is also popular for weddings, and is particularly attractive for mixed Asian and British couples. Anyone who has seen a Vaishnava wedding will know that the priest lights a sacred fire and the bride and groom both place a banana into it towards the end of the ceremony. The banana is an offering to Lord Vishnu.

In 1990, singer and actress Hazel O'Connor married husband Kurt, and the couple duly placed their bananas into the small fire, contained in a pit made of bricks on the temple floor. They smiled for the cameras, and then walked respectfully around the sacred fire. I don't think they were ready for the next day's centre spread in the Sun which read 'WITH THIS BANANA, I THEE WED'. Surely one of the classic headlines of our time! The curious irony is that three years later, one of the paper's executives, a Londoner, married an Asian bride at the temple. An example of the law of karma at work?

Anyone who has been to the tropics will know that there are many varieties of Banana. In England, sadly, we seem to get only two or three types. Our experience with testing is that Banana cakes always turn out well.

Ripe bananas give the best flavour in cake making. Choose fruit that is yellow and slightly flecked with brown. Speed up the ripening, if necessary, by storing in a paper bag at room temperature.

Bhagavat.

Banana Lemon Layered Cake

METRIC	IMP.	US.	
225g	8 oz	2 cups	white self-raising flour
½ tsp.	½ tsp.	½ tsp.	bicarb.
pinch	pinch	pinch	of salt
175g	6 oz	¾ cup	sugar
175g	6 oz	¾ cup	butter
125ml	8 tbs.	½ cup	milk
2	2	2	medium bananas
½ tsp.	½ tsp.	½ tsp.	lemon juice
3	3	3	drops lemon essence

Preheat the oven to 180°C/350°F/Gas mark 4
Use three 15cm/6 inch sandwich tins.

Cream together the butter and the sugar until light and fluffy. Beat thoroughly, stir in the lemon essence and mashed bananas until blended. Sift flour, soda and salt together. Mix milk with lemon juice to sour the milk, then stir both into the creamed mixture until combined.

Grease and line the sandwich tins. Divide the mixture evenly between the three tins. Bake for 25-30 minutes or until light brown. Turn on to wire racks to cool.

Add filling and icing of your choice.

Banana and Walnut Cake

METRIC	IMP.	US.	
200g	7 oz	1 ¾ cups	white self-raising flour
¼ tsp.	¼ tsp.	¼ tsp.	baking powder
¼ tsp.	¼ tsp.	¼ tsp.	bicarb.
pinch	pinch	pinch	salt
100g	4 oz	½ cup	caster sugar
100g	4 oz	½ cup	butter
3 tbs.	3 tbs.	3 tbs.	yoghurt
3	3	3	small bananas
50g	2 oz	½ cup	walnuts, finely chopped

Preheat the oven to 180°C/350°F/Gas mark 4
Use two 23cm/9 inch sandwich tins.

Line and grease the sandwich tins. Sift the flour, baking powder, bicarb and salt into a bowl.

Cream the butter, the yoghurt and sugar until light and creamy. Mash the bananas and mix into the creamed butter. Add the dry ingredients, one third at a time, beating well after each addition.

Stir in the walnuts and spoon into the prepared tin. Bake the cakes for about 30 minutes. Cool on a wire rack.

Banana Almond Loaf

METRIC	IMP.	US.	
225g	8 oz	2 cups	white self-raising flour
½ tsp.	½ tsp.	½ tsp.	baking powder
¾ tsp.	¾ tsp.	¾ tsp.	Salt
100g	4 oz	½ cup	sugar
100g	4 oz	½ cup	butter
2 tbs.	2 tbs.	2 tbs.	milk
4 tbs.	4 tbs.	4 tbs.	sour cream
3	3	3	medium bananas
100g	4 oz	1 cup	chopped almonds
1 tsp.	1 tsp.	1 tsp.	grated orange peel

Preheat the oven to 180°C/350°F/Gas mark 4
Use a 900g/2 lb loaf tin.

Sift together the flour, baking powder and salt. Cream the butter and sugar until light and fluffy. Add sour cream, orange peel, beat well. Mash the bananas, combine with the milk and add to the creamed mixture alternately with the flour mixture. Beat until smooth. Stir in the nuts. Turn into the greased loaf tin. Bake for 45 to 50 minutes. Leave to cool in the tin for 10 minutes, and turn out onto a wire rack.

Banana Teabread

METRIC	IMP.	US.	
225g	8 oz	2 cups	white self-raising flour
½ tsp.	½ tsp.	½ tsp.	baking powder
½ tsp.	½ tsp.	½ tsp.	salt
100g	4 oz	½ cup	caster sugar
6 tbs.	6 tbs.	6 tbs.	butter
4 tbs.	4 tbs.	4 tbs.	sour cream
3	3	3	medium bananas
50g	2 oz	¼ cup	glacé cherries
50g	2 oz	½ cup	walnuts, chopped

Preheat the oven to 180°C/350°F/Gas mark 4
Use a 900g/2 lb loaf tin.

Grease and line the tin. Sift the flour, baking powder and salt. Cream the butter and sugar until light. Add the sour cream and flour. Add the mashed bananas, walnuts and cherries. Spoon into the prepared tin and bake for 1¼ hours. Test with a warm knife and turn out on a rack.

Banana Peanut Loaf

METRIC	IMP.	US.	
175g	6 oz	1 ½ cups	wholemeal self-raising flour
100g	4 oz	1 cup	wheat germ
100g	4 oz	½ cup	brown sugar
250g	9 oz	1 ½ cups	chopped dates
175g	6 oz	¾ cup	butter, melted
300ml	½ pint	1 ¼ cups	of milk
4 tbs.	4 tbs.	4 tbs.	sour cream
3	3	3	medium bananas
50g	2 oz	½ cup	unsalted roasted peanuts

Preheat the oven to 180°C/350°F/Gas mark 4
Use a 900g/2 lb loaf tin.

Grease and line the tin. Sift the flour and wheat germ. Mix in sugar, dates, butter, milk, sour cream and mashed bananas. Pour into the tin, sprinkle with nuts, bake for about 1 ¼ hours. Cool on a rack.

Banana Sour Cream Cake

FOR THE CAKE

METRIC	IMP.	US.	
225g	8 oz	2 cups	white self-raising flour
½ tsp.	½ tsp.	½ tsp.	bicarb.
100g	4 oz	½ cup	castor sugar
175g	6 oz	¾ cup	butter
125ml	8 tbs.	½ cup	of sour cream
1	1	1	meduim banana
1 tsp.	1 tsp.	1 tsp.	Vanilla essence

CAROB ICING;

METRIC	IMP.	US.	
225g	8 oz	2 cups	icing sugar
50g	2 oz	½ cup	carob powder
100g	4 oz	½ cup	cream cheese
2 tbs.	2 tbs.	2 tbs.	butter

Preheat the oven to 180°C/350°F/Gas mark 4
Use a 20cm/8 inch round deep cake tin.

Grease and line the tin. Cream the butter, essence and sugar. Mash the banana and stir in half with half the sour cream and half the dry ingredients. Stir in the remaining banana, sour cream and dry ingredients. Spread into the tin. Bake for 1 ¼ hours. Allow to cool for 10 mins. before turning out on a wire rack.

Carob icing. Beat the cream cheese and butter. Gradually beat in half the sifted icing sugar, the carob then the remaining icing sugar. Beat until thick. Spread over the cold cake.

Turkish Yoghurt Banana Cake

FOR THE CAKE

METRIC	IMP.	US.	
225g	8 oz	2 cups	white self-raising flour
½ tsp.	½ tsp.	½ tsp.	baking powder
pinch	pinch	pinch	salt
100g	4 oz	½ cup	soft brown sugar
100g	4 oz	½ cup	butter
125ml	8 tbs.	½ cup	yoghurt
2	2	2	medium bananas

DECORATION

METRIC	IMP.	US.	
125ml	8 tbs.	½ cup	whipped cream
1	1	1	large banana
2 tbs.	2 tbs.	2 tbs.	coarsely ground walnuts
2 tbs.	2 tbs.	2 tbs.	coarsely ground pistachios

Preheat the oven to 180°C/350°F/Gas mark 4
Use a 20cm/8 inch round cake tin.

Cream the butter and sugar. Add the yoghurt and mix until smooth.

Sift in the flour, baking powder and salt and fold in. Mash the bananas and fold in until evenly blended. Spoon into the greased and floured cake tin and smooth over the surface. Bake for about 40 minutes. Test with a warm knife. Cool for 10 minutes, turn on to a rack and leave until cold.

Slice the cake in half crossways and spread half the whipped cream evenly over the bottom half. Sprinkle the nuts evenly over the cream and then replace the top of the cake. Spread the remaining cream over the top of the cake and, if you wish, decorate with sliced bananas added at the last minute before serving.

Banana and Passion Fruit Cake

FOR THE CAKE;

METRIC	IMP.	US.	
225g	8 oz	2 cups	white self-raising flour
100g	4 oz	½ cup	castor sugar
175g	6 oz	¾ cup	butter
150g	5 oz	½ cup	yoghurt
2	2	2	medium bananas
50g	2 oz	½ cup	chopped walnuts
2	2	2	passion fruit

PASSION FRUIT ICING;

METRIC	IMP.	US.	
225g	8 oz	2 cups	cups icing sugar
1 tsp.	1 tsp.	1 tsp.	soft butter
2	2	2	passion fruit

Preheat the oven to 180°C/350°F/Gas mark 4
Use a 20cm/8 inch deep round cake tin.

Grease and line the cake tin. Cream the butter and sugar until light and fluffy. Mash the bananas and take the pulp out of the passion fruit. Stir in with the walnuts, the yoghurt, and the sifted flour.

Spread the mixture into the prepared tin and bake for about 1 hour. Test with a warm knife. Cool for 10 minutes before turning on to wire rack to cool.

Icing. Sift icing sugar into small heat proof bowl, stir in butter and enough passion fruit pulp to make a stiff paste. Stir over hot water until the icing is spreadable. Spread over the cooled cake.

Banana Cinnamon Cake

FOR THE CAKE.

METRIC	IMP.	US.	
175g	6 oz	1 ½ cups	white self-raising flour
2 tsp.	2 tsp.	2 tsp.	ground cinnamon
100g	4 oz	½ cup	brown sugar
2 tbs.	2 tbs.	2 tbs.	golden syrup
100g	4 oz	½ cup	butter
1 tbs.	1 tbs.	1 tbs.	milk
2 tbs.	2 tbs.	2 tbs.	sour cream
2	2	2	medium bananas

LEMON ICING.

METRIC	IMP.	US.	
225g	8 oz	2 cups	icing sugar
2 tbs.	2 tbs.	2 tbs.	butter
2 tbs.	2 tbs.	2 tbs.	lemon juice, approx.
4 tbs.	4 tbs.	4 tbs.	chopped glacé ginger - optional

Preheat the oven to 180°C/350°F/Gas mark 4
Use a 20cm/8 inch ring tin.

Grease and line the ring tin. Cream the butter, golden syrup and sugar until light and fluffy. Mash the bananas and add along with the sour cream. Mix well. Stir in sifted dry ingredients and milk.

Pour mixture into prepared tin. Bake for about 45 minutes. Test with a warm knife. Cool for 10 minutes before turning on to wire rack to cool.

Lemon Icing. Combine sifted icing sugar with butter and enough juice to mix to a spreadable consistency. Spread over the cold cake. Sprinkle with the finely chopped glacé ginger.

Cottage Cheese Banana Bread

FOR THE CAKE

METRIC	IMP.	US.	
225g	8 oz	2 cups	wholemeal self-raising flour
2 tbs.	2 tbs.	2 tbs.	wheat germ
½ tsp.	½ tsp.	½ tsp.	baking powder
100g	4 oz	½ cup	caster sugar
3 tbs.	3 tbs.	3 tbs.	butter
225g	8 oz	1 cup	cottage cheese
4 tbs.	4 tbs.	4 tbs.	sour cream
3	3	3	small bananas

FOR THE ICING

METRIC	IMP.	US.	
175g	6 oz	1 ½ cups	icing sugar
2	2	2	juice of 2 lemons
1	1	1	rind of 1 lemon

Preheat the oven to 180°C/350°F/Gas mark 4
Use a 450g/1 lb loaf tin.

Grease and line the loaf tin. Sift the flour, wheat germ and baking powder together, adding any bran left in the sieve.

In a separate bowl, cream together the butter, sugar and cottage cheese. Add the sour cream and mix well. Mash the bananas and fold in, alternately with the flour mixture. Pour into the tin. Bake for 1 hour. Turn out onto a wire rack to cool.

Icing. Sieve the icing sugar, and the rind and add enough lemon juice to make a thick icing. Spread over the cake.

Banana and Carrot Bread (Vegan)

METRIC	IMP.	US.	
225g	8 oz	2 cups	wholemeal self-raising flour
2 tbs.	2 tbs.	2 tbs.	soya flour
1 tsp.	1 tsp.	1 tsp.	baking powder
1 tsp.	1 tsp.	1 tsp.	mixed spice
4 tbs.	4 tbs.	4 tbs.	soft brown sugar
100g	4 oz	½ cup	soft vegetable margarine
125ml	8 tbs.	½ cup	soya milk
1	1	1	large banana
1	1	1	medium carrot
2tbs.	2 tbs.	2 tbs.	sesame seeds

Preheat the oven to 180°C/350°F/Gas mark 4
Use a 900g/2 lb loaf tin.

Sieve together the flours, baking powder and mixed spice. Add any separated bran back to the mixture. Cream the margarine and sugar together. Stir in the soya milk, mashed banana and grated carrot, and fold this mixture into the sieved flour. Beat together and then place the mixture into the greased loaf tin. Sprinkle the sesame seeds on top. Bake for about I hour. Test with a warm knife. Turn out on a wire rack to cool.

Liberian Plantain Gingerbread

METRIC	IMP.	US.	
100g	4 oz	½ cup	sugar
1 tsp.	1 tsp.	1 tsp.	ginger
1 tsp.	1 tsp.	1 tsp.	vanilla
1 tsp.	1 tsp.	1 tsp.	cinnamon
¼ tsp.	¼ tsp.	¼ tsp.	clove
2	2	2	half-ripe plantains, sliced
275g	10 oz	2 ½ cups	plain flour
6 tbs.	6 tbs.	6tbs.	molasses
½ tsp.	½ tsp.	½ tsp.	salt
250ml	8 fl. oz	1 cup	sour milk (or buttermilk)
1 ½ tsp.	1 ½ tsp.	1 ½ tsp.	baking powder
¼ tsp.	¼ tsp.	¼ tsp.	nutmeg
100g	4 oz	½ cup	butter
125ml	4 fl. oz	½ cup	water

Preheat the oven to 180°C/350°F/Gas mark 4
Use a 23cm/9 inch square cake tin.

Grease and the cake tin with butter. Make a syrup with the sugar, vanilla, and ½ cup water. Cook the plantains in this syrup lightly. Drain. Slice the plantains into coin-size pieces and spread evenly over the bottom of the buttered cake tin. Sift together all the dry ingredients and spices. Set aside.

Put the butter and molasses into a saucepan and bring to boiling point. Add the sour milk and dry ingredients alternately. Beat vigorously. When smooth, pour the mixture over the plantains in the cake tin. Bake in the preheated oven for 50 to 55 minutes until done. Cool for ten minutes. Turn upside down on serving plate. Cut in squares to serve.

Banana, Nut and Orange Cake (Vegan)

METRIC	IMP.	US.	
150g	5 oz	1 ¼ cups	wholemeal self-raising flour
½ tsp.	½ tsp.	½ tsp.	baking powder
½ tsp.	½ tsp.	½ tsp.	ground cinnamon
100g	4 oz	½ cup	soft brown sugar
225g	8 oz	1 cup	soft vegetable margarine
100g	4 oz	1 cup	ground roasted hazelnuts
225g	8 oz	1 cup	bananas chips
1	1	1	large orange,grated rind.
125ml	8 tbs.	½ cup	orange juice

Preheat the oven to 180°C/350°F/Gas mark 4
Use a 23cm/9 inch cake tin.

Cream the margarine and sugar together until light and fluffy. Sieve together the flour and baking powder in a separate bowl. Fold in the sieved flour and the ground hazelnuts. Add the orange juice, reserving 3 tbs. for the filling. Place half this cake mixture into the greased, lined cake tin. Finely grind the banana chips. Add the reserved orange juice, rind and cinnamon and mix well. Spread this mixture evenly over the cake batter in the tin. Place the remaining half of the cake batter on top and smooth over.

Bake for 1-1 ½ hours. Test with a warm knife. Turn out to cool on a wire rack.

Caramel Banana Cake

FOR THE CAKE;

METRIC	IMP.	US.	
175g	6 oz	1 ½ cups	white self-raising flour
6 tbs.	6 tbs.	6 tbs.	brown sugar
100g	4 oz	½ cup	butter
3 tbs.	3 tbs.	3 tbs.	milk
3	3	3	small bananas

CARAMEL ICING;

METRIC	IMP.	US.	
225g	8 oz	2 cups	icing sugar
6 tbs.	6 tbs.	6 tbs.	butter
100g	4 oz	½ cup	brown sugar
2 tbs.	2 tbs.	2 tbs.	sour cream

Preheat the oven to 180°C/350°F/Gas mark 4
Use a 450g/1 lb loaf tin.

Grease and line the loaf tin. Cream the butter and sugar until light and fluffy. Mash the bananas and stir in. Fold in the sifted dry ingredients and milk. Pour the mixture into the prepared tin and bake for about 1 hour. Allow to stand for 10 minutes before turning on to wire rack to cool.

Caramel Icing. Melt the butter and sugar in saucepan, stirring constantly over the heat without boiling for 2 minutes. Add the sour cream and bring to the boil. Remove from heat and stir in the sifted icing sugar. Allow to cool. Spread the cold cake with icing.

NO MEAT, FISH, EGGS - OR CHOCOLATE

CAKES WITH CAROB.

We adapted most of the cakes in this section from recipes designed for chocolate cakes. Chocolate is one ingredient that you will not find in Hare Krishna kitchens throughout the world, for the simple reason that it contains the stimulant caffeine. There are many good reasons to avoid chocolate and switch to the healthy alternative - carob.

THE DRAWBACKS OF CHOCOLATE.

Chocolate was first cultivated by the Aztecs, and fermented to produce an intoxicating drink called *cacahuatl*. The Spanish brought the drink to Europe, and began to sweeten it with sugar. In the seventeenth century, the drink spread to France and Britain where chocolate houses became popular meeting places. In the nineteenth century, John Fry and John Cadbury separately began the large scale production of drinking chocolate. The drink quickly became a favourite breakfast and bedtime beverage throughout the British empire.

In the present day, those in the developed nations consume large amounts of chocolate and chocolate products. The British are the most avid consumers, munching their way through an average of 7.5kg/16 ½ lb per person each year. The overall European average is 4.8kg/10 ½ lb.

Chocolate contains caffeine and theobromine, both stimulants that act directly on the brain. Although caffeine has pain killing properties, doctors avoided it because of numerous acknowledged side effects. These include anxiety, nervousness, tension, nausea and sometimes heart palpitations. Caffeine increases the pulse in most individuals. Recent research has shown that over-stimulation of the digestive system by caffeine can lead to 'leaching' of water soluble vitamins B and C. Caffeine is associated with high levels of blood cholesterol, one of the major factors in heart disease.

Doctors in America and Europe advise pregnant mothers to limit their intake of coffee due to its well-known caffeine content. Caffeine and theobromine have been linked to benign breast disease, causing painful swellings for many teenage girls.

Perhaps the most well known side effect of chocolate is teenage acne, caused by the presence of oxalic acid, which lowers the body calcium level. Oxalic acid is also associated with the formation of kidney stones.

Chocolate is near the top of the table of common food allergens. Migraine sufferers avoid chocolate due to the presence of phenylethylamine and tyramine, substances both known to trigger attacks.

CAROB, THE NATURAL ALTERNATIVE.

Carob contains none of the harmful substances in Chocolate. It is naturally sweeter and does not require the addition of large amounts of refined sugar. Carob is richer in fibre, vitamins and minerals.

The carob tree is a member of the legume or pea family. It originates in the Mediterranean area, where locals know it as Locust Bean. Many believe that the 'locusts' which John the Baptist ate in the wilderness where actually carob pods, hence the alternative name - St John's bread.

The carob tree was imported into the United States in 1854, and is now common throughout that country. The worlds largest grower is Spain, with 200,000 tons of the bean produced each year. Cyprus, Italy and Greece follow close behind.

The carob tree grows best in dry regions, below an altitude of 500 metres. It is not prone to fungus or disease, and is thus generally free of chemical spraying. The tree takes 15 years to begin regular production of the fruit.

The developing carob pods at first resemble broad beans, but as they mature, they turn a dark chocolate brown colour with a glossy surface. The pods are 10 - 18cm/4 - 8 inches long and about 2.5 - 5cm/1 - 2 inches wide. The sweet flesh contains 4 - 12 extremely hard brown beans.

The seeds and pods are separated, and the seeds used to produce locust bean gum, an essential ingredient of most mass produced ice cream. The pods are then roasted, milled and sieved to produce carob powder.

CAROB IN COOKING.

Carob powder can be used directly in place of cocoa, and dark and light carob bars can replace chocolate, weight for weight. Carob chips are available from many wholefood shops, and these can be used weight for weight as the carob bars. Carob is easier to melt for dipping and spreading than chocolate, although it does not produce the same kind of smooth sheen. Carob can be used in hot and cold drinks, puddings and ice cream.

Carob powder should be sieved, like flour, before use. This will eliminate lumps, and help to introduce more air into the cake. Care should be taken when introducing carob into the bowl of an electric mixer. It is less dense than cocoa, and more likely to cause a dust storm in the kitchen.

Carob, Cheese and Walnut Cake

METRIC	IMP.	US.	
175g	6 oz	1 ½ cups	white self-raising flour
¼ tsp.	¼ tsp.	¼ tsp.	baking powder
50g	2 oz	½ cup	carob powder
100g	4 oz	½ cup	brown sugar
100g	4 oz	½ cup	butter
5 tbs.	5 tbs.	5 tbs.	milk
175g	6 oz	¾ cup	packaged cream cheese
4 tbs.	4 tbs.	4 tbs.	sour cream
100g	4 oz	1 cup	chopped walnuts

Preheat the oven to 180°C/350°F/Gas mark 4
Use a 20cm/8 inch ring tin.

Grease the ring tin. Cream the butter, cream cheese and sugar until light and fluffy. Beat in the sour cream and mix well. Stir in the walnuts, then half the sifted flour with the carob, the baking powder and half the milk. Stir in the remaining flour and milk. Spread into the prepared tin. Bake for about 40 minutes. Test with a warm knife. Allow to stand for 10 minutes before turning out on a wire rack. Dust with sifted icing sugar before serving.

Carob Ripple Cake

METRIC	IMP.	US.	
225g	8 oz	2 cups	white self-raising flour
½ tsp.	½ tsp.	½ tsp.	baking powder
3 tbs.	3 tbs.	3 tbs.	carob powder
100g	4 oz	½ cup	caster sugar
100g	4 oz	½ cup	butter
6 tbs.	6 tbs.	6 tbs.	sour cream
125ml	8 tbs.	½ cup	milk

Preheat the oven to 180°C/350°F/Gas mark 4
Use a 20cm/8 inch baba tin.

Grease the baba tin. Cream the butter and sugar until light and fluffy. Whisk in the sour cream and mix well. Transfer the mixture to large bowl. Stir in half the sifted flour, the baking powder and 2 tbs. of milk, then stir in remaining flour and another 2 tbs. of milk. Blend the carob with the remaining 4 tbs. of milk. Stir until smooth with 2 tbs. of the cake mixture. Fold the carob mixture lightly through the cake mixture to give a rippled effect. Spoon into the prepared tin, smoothing the top slightly. Bake for about 40 minutes. Turn on to wire rack to cool. Dust with icing sugar before serving.

Apricot Carob Chip Cake

METRIC	IMP.	US.	
175g	6 oz	1 ½ cups	white self-raising flour
100g	4 oz	½ cup	caster sugar
100g	4 oz	1 cup	desiccated coconut
100g	4 oz	½ cup	butter
100g	4 oz	¾ cup	carob chips
2 tbs.	2 tbs.	2 tbs.	sour cream
75g	3 oz	½ cup	chopped dried apricots
300ml	½ pint	1 ¼ cups	apricot nectar

Preheat the oven to 150°C/300°F/Gas mark 2
Use a deep 20cm/8 inch round cake tin.

Grease the cake tin. Combine the apricots and nectar in a bowl and stand for an hour. Cream together the butter and sugar until light and fluffy. Stir in the sour cream and coconut. Mix thoroughly, adding the flour, then the apricot mixture. Mix well, adding the carob chips. Spread in the prepared tin and bake for 1 and ¼ hours. Dust with sifted icing sugar when cool.

Carob Peppermint Cake

FOR THE CAKE

METRIC	IMP.	US.	
150g	5 oz	1 ¼ cups	white self-raising flour
4 tbs.	4 tbs.	4 tbs.	carob powder
½ tsp.	½ tsp.	½ tsp.	bicarb.
175g	6 oz	¾ cup	brown sugar
100g	4 oz	½ cup	butter
100g	4 oz	¾ cup	carob chips or bar
125ml	8 tbs.	½ cup	milk
4 tbs.	4 tbs.	4 tbs.	sour cream
5 tbs.	5 tbs.	5 tbs.	water

PEPPERMINT CREAM

METRIC	IMP.	US.	
175g	6 oz	¾ cup	butter
500g	18 oz	4 ½ cups	icing sugar
1 tbs.	1 tbs.	1 tbs.	milk
½ tsp.	½ tsp.	½ tsp.	peppermint essence

CAROB ICING

METRIC	IMP.	US.	
225g	8 oz	2 cups	icing sugar
2 tbs.	2 tbs.	2 tbs.	carob powder
1 tsp.	1 tsp.	1 tsp.	butter
5 tbs.	5 tbs.	5 tbs.	hot water

Preheat the oven to 180°C/350°F/Gas mark 4
Use a 23cm/9 inch square slab tin.

Grease and line the cake tin. Melt the carob chips with the water in heatproof bowl over hot water, cool to room temperature.

Beat together the ingredients, except the carob, in large bowl. A carob to the mixture. Beat vigorously for about 3 minutes or until mixture changes in colour and becomes smooth. Pour into the prepared tin, bake for about 40 minutes. Stand 5 minutes before turning on to wire rack to cool. Spread the cold cake with the peppermint cream. Refrigerate for one hour. Spread the icing over the cream, then refrigerate until set.

Peppermint Cream: Cream butter until light and fluffy, gradually beat in sifted icing sugar, then milk and essence.

Carob Icing: Sift icing sugar and carob powder into a bowl, stir in the combined butter and water. Beat until smooth.

Carob Cherry Cake (Vegan)

METRIC	IMP.	US.	
225g	8 oz	2 cups	white self-raising flour
175g	6 oz	¾ cup	brown sugar
50g	2 oz	½ cup	carob powder
1 tsp.	1 tsp.	1 tsp.	baking powder
½ tsp.	½ tsp.	½ tsp.	salt
100g	4 oz	½ cup	vegetable oil
100g	4 oz	½ cup	preserved cherries
75g	3 oz	¾ cup	chopped almonds
1 tsp.	1 tsp.	1 tsp.	lemon juice
½ tsp.	½ tsp.	½ tsp.	vanilla

Preheat the oven to 180°C/350°F/Gas mark 4
Use a 20cm/8 inch square cake tin.

Grease and line the baking tin. Mix the flour, sugar, carob, baking powder, salt and almonds. Add enough water to the cherry syrup to make one cup. Stir syrup-water and the remaining ingredients into the flour mixture. Pour into the cake tin and bake for 35 to 40 minutes or until a warm knife inserted in the middle comes out clean. Sprinkle with icing sugar if desired.

rob Sponge Cake

		US.	
	oz	2 cups	white self-raising flour
	½ tsp.	½ tsp.	bicarb.
	½ tsp.	½ tsp.	baking powder
50g	2 oz	½ cup	carob powder
175g	6 oz	¾ cup	butter
400g	14 oz	1 cup	sweetened condensed milk
1 tsp.	1 tsp.	1 tsp.	vanilla essence
125ml	8 tbs.	½ cup	warm water

Preheat the oven to 180°C/350°F/Gas mark 4
Use a 23cm/9 inch round cake tin.

Grease and line the cake tin. Sieve all the dry ingredients. Mix the condensed milk, warm water and vanilla essence together. Rub the butter into the flour until it resembles fine breadcrumbs. Pour the wet mixture into the dry and mix thoroughly. Pour into the prepared tin and bake for 40-45 minutes. Let the cake cool in the tin before turning out.

Variations.

For a plain sponge cake, substitute 50g/2 oz/½ cup cornflour for the 50g/2 oz/½ cup carob powder.

For a custard sponge cake, substitute 50g/2 oz/½ cup custard powder for the 50g/2 oz/½ cup carob powder.

For a coffee sponge cake, 50g/2 oz/½ cup decaff. coffee powder for the 50g/2 oz/½ cup carob powder.

Swedish Carob Cake

METRIC	IMP.	US.	
200g	7 oz	1 ¾ cups	white self raising flour
2 tbs.	2 tbs.	2 tbs.	potato flour
1 tsp.	1 tsp.	1 tsp.	baking powder
50g	2 oz	½ cup	carob powder
¼ tsp.	¼ tsp.	¼ tsp.	salt
100g	4 oz	½ cup	caster sugar
6 tbs.	6 tbs.	6 tbs.	butter, at room temperature
125ml	8 tbs.	½ cup	buttermilk
4 tbs.	4 tbs.	4 tbs.	sour cream
3 tbs.	3 tbs.	3 tbs.	blanched almonds, chopped
1 tsp.	1 tsp.	1 tsp.	vanilla sugar
4 tbs.	4 tbs.	4 tbs.	chopped candied orange peel
6 tbs.	6 tbs.	6 tbs.	boiling water

Preheat the oven to 180°C/350°F/Gas mark 4
Use an 18cm/7 inch cake tin.

Grease and line the cake tin. Cream together the butter and sugar until pale and fluffy. Add the sour cream, vanilla sugar, orange peel and almonds and mix well. Blend the carob and boiling water and stir into the mixture.

Sift together the baking powder, salt, potato flour and self-raising flour. Stir the dry ingredients into the mixture alternately with the buttermilk.

Turn the mixture into the prepared cake tin and bake for 1 hour or until a warm knife inserted into the centre comes out clean.

Carob Orange Sponge

FOR THE CAKE

METRIC	IMP.	US.	
100g	4 oz	1 cup	white self-raising white flour
50g	2 oz	½ cup	All-Bran
100g	4 oz	½ cup	caster sugar
100g	4 oz	½ cup	butter
125ml	8 tbs.	½ cup	orange juice
1 tsp.	1 tsp.	1 tsp.	grated orange rind

DECORATION

METRIC	IMP.	US.	
75g	3 oz	½ cup	carob chips or bar
250ml	8 fl. oz	1 cup	double cream
3 tbs.	3 tbs.	3 tbs.	jelly-type orange marmalade

Preheat the oven to 180°C/350°F/Gas mark 4
Use two 18cm/7 inch sandwich tins.

Grease and line the sandwich tins. Put the bran into a basin, add the orange juice and allow to stand for 30 minutes.

Cream together the butter, sugar and orange rind until soft and light. Add four tbs. of the double cream to the mixture. Sift the flour into the mixture then add the soaked bran with any orange juice left. Fold gently and carefully into the creamed mixture. Divide the mixture between the prepared tins and bake just above the centre of the oven for approximately 25 minutes or until firm to the touch. Turn the sponges out of the tins and allow to cool.

Cover one sponge with the marmalade; whip the remainder of the cream, spread a little over the marmalade, top with the second sponge. Melt the carob chips or bar in a basin over hot water; spread over the top of the sponge and decorate with the remaining cream.

Carob Almond Cake

FOR THE CAKE

METRIC	IMP.	US.	
100g	4 oz	1 cup	white self-raising white flour
½ tsp.	½ tsp.	½ tsp.	baking powder
50g	2 oz	½ cup	carob powder
1 tbs.	1 tbs.	1 tbs.	dry instant decaff.coffee
100g	4 oz	½ cup	castor sugar
100g	4 oz	½ cup	butter
250ml	8 fl. oz	1 cup	sour cream
75g	3 oz	¾ cup	packaged ground almonds
1 tbs.	1 tbs.	1 tbs.	toasted flaked almonds
2 tsp.	2 tsp.	2 tsp.	vanilla essence

CAROB ICING

METRIC	IMP.	US.	
75g	3 oz	¾ cup	icing sugar
2 tbs.	2 tbs.	2 tbs.	carob powder
2 tsp.	2 tsp.	2 tsp.	dry instant decaffeinated coffee
6 tbs.	6 tbs.	6 tbs.	butter
2 tbs.	2 tbs.	2 tbs.	boiling water

Preheat the oven to 180°C/350°F/Gas mark 4
Use a 20cm/8 inch ring tin.

Grease and line the ring tin. Dissolve the coffee in water, blend with the sifted carob. Cream the butter, essence and sugar in small bowl with until light and fluffy, whisk in the sour cream. Transfer to a large bowl, stir in ground almonds, then the sifted flour and carob mixture. Spread into prepared tin. Bake for about 40 minutes. Stand for five minutes before turning on to a wire rack to cool.

Icing: Combine sifted icing sugar and carob in bowl with butter, stir in combined coffee and water. Spread the cold cake with icing and sprinkle with flaked almonds.

erican Fudge Cake.

FOR THE CAKE

	MP.	US.	
175g	6 oz	1 ½ cups	white self-raising flour
1 tsp.	1 tsp.	1 tsp.	baking powder
50g	2 oz	½ cup	carob powder
100g	4 oz	½ cup	dark soft brown sugar
100g	4 oz	½ cup	butter
125ml	8 tbs.	½ cup	sour cream

CAROB FILLING

METRIC	IMP.	US.	
2 tbs.	2 tbs.	2 tbs.	carob powder
150g	5 oz	1 ¼ cup	icing sugar, sieved
100g	4 oz	½ cup	butter
2	2	2	drops of vanilla essence

CAROB ICING

METRIC	IMP.	US.	
2 tbs.	2 tbs.	2 tbs.	carob powder
225g	8 oz	1 ¼ cups	carob chips or bar
125ml	8 tbs.	½ cup	double cream

Preheat the oven to 190°C/375°F/Gas mark 5
Use two 20cm/8 inch cake tins.

Grease and line the cake tins. Cream together the butter and sugar. Gradually beat in the sour cream. Sieve together the dry ingredients and fold them into the mixture. Divide the mixture equally between the tins. Bake for 30-35 minutes, until cooked. Turn out on to a wire tray to cool.

Make the filling by mixing the carob with 2 tbs. of boiling water to a smooth paste. Allow to cool. Beat together the butter, sieved icing sugar and essence, until light and fluffy. Beat in the carob. Slice the cake in half and then sandwich the halves together with the filling.

For the icing, melt the carob chips or bar carefully over water. Make the carob powder into a paste with water as before and mix with the melted bar. Slowly whisk in the cream until smooth and thickened. Spread the icing evenly over the cake with a cake slice. Serve hot with whipped cream or ice-cream.

Turkish Carob Cake

METRIC	IMP.	US.	
225g	8 oz	2 cups	white self-raising flour
1 tsp.	1 tsp.	1 tsp.	baking powder
¼ tsp.	¼ tsp.	¼ tsp.	ground nutmeg
100g	4 oz	½ cup	butter
225g	8 oz	1 cup	caster sugar
100g	4 oz	¾ cup	carob chips or bar
250ml	8 fl. oz	1 cup	yoghurt
			apricot jam for filling

Preheat the oven to 180°C/350°F/Gas mark 4
Use a 20cm/8 inch round cake tin.

Grease and line the cake tin. Cream together the butter and sugar until light and fluffy. Melt the carob bar or chips in a bowl over hot water. Leave to cool a little and then add to the cake mixture and stir until well blended. Stir in the yoghurt. Sift together the flour, baking powder and nutmeg. Add to the other ingredients and mix thoroughly.

Pour into the prepared cake tin and bake in the preheated oven for about 40 minutes or until a warm knife inserted into the centre comes out clean. Cool in tin for 15 minutes and then turn out on to a wire rack and leave until cold. Slice in half crossways and sandwich together with jam.

Carob Lime Cake

FOR THE CAKE

METRIC	IMP.	US.	
150g	5 oz	1 ¼ cups	white self-raising flour
3 tbs.	3 tbs.	3 tbs.	carob powder
50g	2 oz	½ cup	desiccated coconut
6 tbs.	6 tbs.	6 tbs.	caster sugar
6 tbs.	6 tbs.	6 tbs.	soft butter
4 tbs.	4 tbs.	4 tbs.	sour cream
2	2	2	limes, grated rind and juice
125ml	8 tbs.	½ cup	milk

FOR THE SYRUP

METRIC	IMP.	US.	
6 tbs.	6 tbs.	6 tbs.	caster sugar
4 tbs.	4 tbs.	4 tbs.	lime cordial

Preheat the oven to 180°C/350°F/Gas mark 4
Use a 900g/2 lb loaf tin.

Grease and line the loaf tin. Cream the butter and sugar together, and gradually beat in the sour cream. Beat in the coconut and lime juice; fold in the flour, carob powder and lime rind. Mix in the milk. Spoon the mixture into the tin, making the surface level, then bake for about 55 minutes. Test with a warm knife. Carefully lift out with the paper and cool. Clean the tin.

For the syrup, dissolve the sugar in the cordial over a gentle heat and when dissolved and clear, bring to the boil for 2 or 3 minutes till it forms a thin syrup. Return the cake to the tin and pour the syrup over, poking it in with a skewer. Cool the cake in the tin.

Carob and Orange Cake

FOR THE CAKE

METRIC	IMP.	US.	
225g	8 oz	2 cups	white self-raising flour
½ tsp.	½ tsp.	½ tsp.	baking powder
75g	3 oz	¾ cup	carob powder
100g	4 oz	½ cup	caster sugar
100g	4 oz	½ cup	unsalted butter
300ml	½ pint	1 ¼ cups	buttermilk

FILLING, ICING AND DECORATION

METRIC	IMP.	US.	
225g	8 oz	2 cups	icing sugar, sifted
2 tbs.	2 tbs	2 tbs.	unsalted butter
1	1	1	grated rind of 1 orange
1	1	1	juice of 1 orange
			fresh orange segments

Preheat the oven to 180°C/350°F/Gas mark 4
Use two 20cm/8 inch sandwich tins.

Grease and line the sandwich tins. Sift together the flour and carob. Cream the butter and sugar until light and fluffy. Stir in the buttermilk. Fold in the flour and carob. Turn the mixture into the prepared tins and bake for about 40 minutes. Remove from the oven and allow to cool in the tins for 5 minutes. Turn out on to a wire rack and leave to cool. When cold, split each cake into two layers.

Icing: Cream the butter with the orange rind until soft. Gradually beat in the icing sugar, alternately with the orange juice. Use some of the butter icing to sandwich the cakes together. Spread the remaining butter icing over the top and sides of the cake. Decorate the top of the cake with the orange segments.

a's Food Carob Cake

FOR THE CAKE

ME.	IMP.	US.	
200g	7 oz	1 ¾ cups	white self raising flour
50g	2 oz	½ cup	carob powder
1 tsp.	1 tsp.	1 tsp.	baking powder
100g	4 oz	½ cup	dark brown sugar
1 tbs.	1 tbs.	1 tbs.	golden syrup
100g	4 oz	½ cup	butter
100g	4 oz	¾ cup	carob chips or bar
4 tbs.	4 tbs.	4 tbs.	sour cream
125ml	8 tbs.	½ cup	milk

Preheat the oven to 180°C/350°F/Gas mark 4
Use two 20cm/8 inch sandwich tins.

Line the base and grease the sandwich tins. Heat the carob chips or chopped carob bar in a saucepan with the butter, sugar and syrup until just melted. Sift the flour, carob powder and baking powder into a mixing bowl. Make a well in the centre and stir in the cooled melted ingredients. Stir in the sour cream and beat well, then mix in the milk. Pour the mixture into the prepared tins and bake in the preheated oven for 30 minutes or until set. Allow to cool in the tins for ten minutes before turning out on to a wire rack to cool completely.

Quick Carob Sandwich Cake

FOR THE CAKE

METRIC	IMP.	US.	
175g	6 oz	1 ½ cups	white self raising flour
50g	2 oz	½ cup	carob powder
1 tsp.	1 tsp.	1 tsp.	baking powder
4 tbs.	4 tbs.	4 tbs.	sugar
2 tbs.	2 tbs	2 tbs.	golden syrup
4 tbs.	4 tbs.	4 tbs.	butter
300ml	½ pint	1 ¼ cups	milk
1 tbs.	1 tbs.	1 tbs.	lemon juice
¼ tsp.	¼ tsp.	¼ tsp.	vanilla essence
1 tbs.	1 tbs.	1 tbs.	water

TO FINISH:

			raspberry jam
			icing sugar

Preheat the oven to 220°C/425°F/Gas mark 7
Use two 18cm/7 inch sandwich tins.

Grease the sandwich tins. Melt the butter and syrup in the milk in a saucepan over moderate heat. Mix well and cool.

Sift the dry ingredients into a mixing bowl. Pour in the cooled liquid and beat well. Add the lemon juice, water and vanilla, then beat again. Pour the mixture into the sandwich tins. Spread out evenly. Bake in the centre of the preheated oven for 15 to 20 minutes. Remove from the oven and cool on a wire rack. Sandwich together with raspberry jam and sprinkle the top with icing sugar sifted through a paper doily.

MAKING LEMON JUICE FOR KRISHNA.

CAKES WITH CITRUS FRUITS.

I came to Bhaktivedanta Manor in 1984. I had some interest in Krishna Consciousness, but it was not easy to make the transition from the whimsical life of a socialist/anarchist poet to that of a strict Vaishnava student, or brahmacari. I liked the friendliness of the temple residents, and I began to feel that I could fit in. My real commitment to this new lifestyle came as I was working in the kitchen.

The Vaishnava way of life involves a certain amount of fasting and feasting. Festival days fall throughout the year. In October 1984, we celebrated the birth of the father of Srila Prabhupada's spiritual master. My job was to make a drink called nimbu pani, with the juice of hundreds of lemons. When I saw the fruit boxes stacked up, I was ready to ready to pick up my guitar and hit the road, with a 'thank you very much and Hare Krishna'.

Partha, the head cook, was a larger-than-life, jovial sort of person and I think his smile was what convinced me to pick up the first lemon. For the rest of the morning, I squeezed and squeezed and squeezed. Somehow, I began to enjoy it. The atmosphere in the kitchen was lively and warm. There were a dozen of us, engaged in different tasks. Some chopping vegetables and fruit, others preparing dough and frying puris in hot ghee. Partha oversaw the operation while stirring a huge bubbling pot of vegetable subji. Outside the steamed up windows, the English rain lashed the courtyard. I felt that I was among true friends. We laughed and spoke of our different routes to Bhaktivedanta Manor. I felt a real bond with those devotees. My conviction was no longer on the intellectual platform. It became tangible, I could taste it. It was heartfelt.

Bhagavat.

Vegan Lemon Cake

METRIC	IMP.	US.	
225g	8 oz	2 cups	wholemeal self-raising flour
1 tsp.	1 tsp.	1 tsp.	baking powder
100g	4 oz	½ cup	demerara sugar
175g	6 oz	¾ cup	vegetable margarine
125ml	8 tbs.	½ cup	hot water
2 tbs.	2 tbs.	2 tbs.	malt extract
2	2	2	lemons

Preheat the oven to 200°C/400°F/Gas mark 6
Use two 23cm/9 inch sandwich tins.

Sift the flour and baking powder into a bowl, add the sugar and mix well by lifting and sprinkling, using a spoon. Put the margarine to melt in a small saucepan over a low heat. Remove from heat as soon as it's melted.

Put the hot water in a jug together with the malt extract and set aside. Finely grate the lemon rinds, add to the dry ingredients and mix in by lifting and sprinkling as before. Squeeze the lemons, add the juice to the water and malt mixture and stir until the malt has completely dissolved.

Preheat the oven and prepare the tins by lightly greasing and flouring them. As quickly as you can, add the melted margarine to the dry ingredients and stir well in, followed immediately by the water, malt and lemon juice mixture. Beat well for a few moments only before transferring equal amounts to each of the two prepared sponge tins and placing them in the preheated oven. Bake till the top goes firm and golden brown (about 20-25 minutes), or test with a warm knife. Allow to cool before removing from the tins.

Tangy Citrus Cake

METRIC	IMP.	US.	
200g	7 oz	1 ¾ cups	white self-raising flour
¼ tsp.	¼ tsp.	¼ tsp.	salt
6 tbs.	6 tbs.	6 tbs.	sugar
6 tbs.	6 tbs.	6 tbs.	butter
1	1	1	rind and juice of lemon
4 tbs.	4 tbs.	4 tbs.	sour cream
125ml	8 tbs.	½ cup	milk
			butter for greasing

Preheat the oven to 180°C/350°F/Gas mark 4
Use a 15cm/6 inch cake tin.

Line and grease the cake tin. Mix the flour and salt in a mixing bowl. Rub in the butter until the mixture resembles fine breadcrumbs. Add the sugar and grated citrus rind. In a bowl, mix the sour cream with 30 ml/2 tbs. of the milk and stir into the flour mixture. Gradually add the citrus juice, beating vigorously. If necessary, add the remaining milk to give a consistency that just drops off the end of a wooden spoon.

Spoon the mixture into the cake tin and bake for 1-1 ½ hours or until cooked through. Cool on a wire rack.

Citrus Sour Cream Cake

METRIC	IMP.	US.	
225g	8 oz	2 cups	white self-raising flour
100g	4 oz	½ cup	caster sugar
100g	4 oz	½ cup	butter
125ml	8 tbs.	½ cup	sour cream
75g	3 oz	½ cup	mixed peel

Preheat the oven to 160°C/325°F/Gas mark 3
Use a 900g/2 lb loaf tin.

Grease the loaf tin, line with greaseproof paper and grease the paper. Cream butter and sugar in a small bowl until light and fluffy. Stir in mixed peel, flour and sour cream and mix well. Spread mixture into prepared tin. Bake the oven for 1¼ hours. Stand for 5 minutes before turning onto wire rack to cool. Dust with icing sugar before serving.

Orange Teabread

Mandarins or tangerines could be used in place of oranges. Orange juice and milk mixed together may curdle, but do not worry because it does not affect the texture in any way.

METRIC	*IMP.*	*US.*	
225g	8 oz	2 cups	white self-raising flour
½ tsp.	½ tsp.	½ tsp.	baking powder
100g	4 oz	½ cup	caster sugar
100g	4 oz	1 cup	butter
4 tbs.	4 tbs.	4 tbs.	sour cream
125ml	8 tbs.	½ cup	milk
2 tbs.	2 tbs.	2 tbs.	orange juice
			finely grated rind of 1 orange

Preheat the oven to 190°C/375°F/Gas mark 5
Use a 900g/2 lb loaf tin.

Line and grease the loaf tin. Cream together the butter and sugar. Gradually add the sour cream. Fold in the sifted flour with baking powder. Mix together, juice, rind and milk. Add to flour mixture, beating well. Turn into prepared tin and bake for 40-45 minutes. Turn out and cool on wire rack.

Orange Sponge Cake

FOR THE CAKE;

METRIC	IMP.	US.	
225g	8 oz	2 cups	white self-raising flour
100g.	4 oz.	½ cup	caster sugar
100g.	4 oz.	1 cup	soft butter
125ml	8 tbs.	½ cup	sour cream
			grated rind of 2 small oranges
			icing sugar, to dust

ORANGE BUTTER CREAM;

METRIC	IMP.	US.	
100g	4 oz	1 cup	icing sugar, sieved
3 tbs.	3 tbs.	3 tbs.	butter
			grated rind of 1 orange

Preheat the oven to 180°C/350°F/Gas mark 4
Use two 20cm/8 inch sandwich tins.

Grease and line the sandwich tins with greased greaseproof paper. Measure all the cake ingredients into a bowl and beat well for about 2 minutes until thoroughly blended. Divide the mixture between the two tins and level out evenly.

Bake in the oven for about 35 minutes until the sponges shrink away from the sides of the tin and turn a golden brown colour. Leave to cool in the tins for a 10 minutes then turn out, peel off paper and finish cooling on a wire rack.

Butter cream: Measure the ingredients into a bowl and cream together until blended, adding a little orange juice to soften the mixture if necessary. Use to sandwich the two cakes together. Serve dusted with a little icing sugar.

Glazed Lemon Cake

FOR THE CAKE

METRIC	IMP.	US.	
175g	6 oz	1 ½ cups	white self-raising flour
1 tsp.	1 tsp.	1 tsp.	salt
6 tbs.	6 tbs.	6 tbs.	caster sugar
6 tbs.	6 tbs.	6 tbs.	soft butter
4 tbs.	4 tbs.	4 tbs.	sour cream
125ml	8 tbs.	½ cup	milk
100g	4 oz	1 cup	walnuts, chopped
			finely grated rind of 2 lemons

GLAZE

METRIC	IMP.	US.	
175g	6 oz	¾ cup	sugar
3 tbs.	3 tbs.	3 tbs.	fresh lemon juice

Preheat the oven to 180°C/350°F/Gas mark 4
Use a 450g/1 lb loaf tin.

Beat together butter, sour cream and sugar until fluffy. Stir in rind. Sift together flour and salt and add to the butter mixture. Add the milk, a little at a time. Stir in nuts and pour into the greased loaf tin. Bake for about an hour, until the cake rises and the top is firm and browned. Cool in the tin for twenty minutes. Remove from the tin to a cooling rack.

Glaze: Stir the ingredients together over a medium heat until the sugar has melted, then pour over cake, decorating top with walnut halves.

Lime Buttermilk Cake

FOR THE CAKE

METRIC	IMP.	US.	
225g	8 oz	2 cups	white self raising flour
½ tsp.	½ tsp.	½ tsp.	baking powder
100g	4 oz	½ cup	caster sugar
100g	4 oz	½ cup	butter
6 tbs.	6 tbs.	6 tbs.	sour cream
300ml	½ pint	1 ¼ cups	buttermilk
1 tbs.	1 tbs.	1 tbs.	grated lime rind

LIME SYRUP

METRIC	IMP.	US.	
175g	6 oz	¾ cup	sugar
125ml	8 tbs.	½ cup	lime juice.
5 tbs.	5 tbs.	5 tbs.	water

Preheat the oven to 180°C/350°F/Gas mark 4
Use a 20cm/8 inch ring tin.

Grease and lightly flour the ring tin, shaking out excess flour. Cream the butter, rind and sugar in small bowl with until light and fluffy. Whisk in sour cream, beat until combined. Transfer mixture to large bowl, stir in half the flour, the baking powder and half the buttermilk, then stir in the remaining flour and buttermilk.

Spread the mixture into the prepared tin. Bake for about 1 hour. Stand for five minutes before turning out on a wire rack. Pour hot lime syrup evenly over the cake.

Lime Syrup: Combine lime juice, sugar and water in saucepan. Stir over the heat until the sugar dissolves. Bring to the boil; remove from heat.

Jewish Orange Cake.

METRIC	IMP.	US.	
225g	8 oz	2 cups	white self-raising flour, sifted
¼ tsp.	¼ tsp.	¼ tsp.	bicarb.
½ tsp.	½ tsp.	½ tsp.	baking powder
175g	6 oz	¾ cup	sugar
175g	6 oz	¾ cup	butter
125ml	8 tbs.	½ cup	milk
75g	3 oz	½ cup	currants
50g	2 oz	½ cup	walnuts
1	1	1	orange, squeezed
4 tbs.	4 tbs.	4 tbs.	yoghurt
5 tbs.	5 tbs.	5 tbs.	orange juice
1 tbs.	1 tbs.	1 tbs.	lemon juice
1 tsp.	1 tsp.	1 tsp.	ground cinnamon

Preheat the oven to 180°C/350°F/Gas mark 4
Use a 20cm/8 inch round cake tin.

Cut the squeezed orange into pieces, place in a blender and reduce to a pulp. Scrape into a bowl. Now blend the currants, and then the nuts, and add both to the bowl. Mix them thoroughly.

Mix the flour, bicarb, baking powder and the sugar (reserve 2 tbs.) together in a large bowl. Add the butter and three quarters of the milk and work together for about 2 minutes or until light and smooth. Add the remaining milk, yoghurt and cinnamon. Beat for a further 2 minutes. Stir in the orange-nut mixture until evenly distributed.

Grease and flour the cake tin and pour in the mixture. Bake for about 50 minutes. Remove from the oven and immediately pour over the mixed orange and lemon juices. Mix the remaining sugar with the cinnamon and sprinkle it over the surface. Leave until cold before serving.

Californian Orange Cake

METRIC	IMP.	US.	
225g	8 oz	2 cups	white self-raising flour
¼ tsp.	¼ tsp.	¼ tsp.	bicarb.
¼ tsp.	¼ tsp.	¼ tsp.	baking powder
¼ tsp.	¼ tsp.	¼ tsp.	salt
100g	4 oz	½ cup	caster sugar
175g	6 oz	¾ cup	butter, softened
2 tbs.	2 tbs.	2 tbs.	sour cream
300ml	½ pint	1 ¼ cups	buttermilk
½ tsp.	½ tsp.	½ tsp.	vanilla essence
1 tsp.	1 tsp.	1 tsp.	ground cinnamon
1	1	1	large orange
100g	4 oz	1 cup	chopped walnuts
175g	6 oz	1 cup	sultanas
50g	2 oz	½ cup	desiccated coconut

Preheat the oven to 180°C/350°F/Gas mark 4
Use a 23cm/9 inch square cake tin.

Line the base of the cake tin and grease well. Beat the butter and sugar until creamy. Add the sour cream and vanilla essence, and beat well. Sift the dry ingredients together, and fold in with the buttermilk.

Peel the orange, removing as much of the white pith as possible; chop very finely and mix in a bowl with the chopped nuts and sultanas. Spoon out one-quarter to one-third of this mixture and mix it into the cake mixture. To the remaining orange-nuts-sultana mixture, add the coconut, and set aside. Spoon the mixture into the cake tin, and bake for 40 to 45 minutes. Remove from the oven and stand for 5 minutes.

Preheat the grill. Carefully spread the reserved orange-nuts-sultana mixture over the top of the cake, and toast. Remove from heat and allow to stand for a further 5 minutes. Then carefully turn out onto a cake rack which has been covered with greaseproof paper. Reverse the cake to top side uppermost and allow to cool.

Passion Fruit and Orange Cake

METRIC	IMP.	US.	
175g	6 oz	1 ½ cups	white self-raising flour
100g	4 oz	½ cup	caster sugar
100g	4 oz	½ cup	butter
6 tbs.	6 tbs.	6 tbs.	sour cream
225g	8 oz	1 cup	dried mixed fruit
5 tbs.	5 tbs.	5 tbs.	orange juice
125ml	8 tbs.	½ cup	strained passion fruit juice
1 tsp.	1 tsp.	1 tsp.	mixed spice

Preheat the oven to 160°C/325°F/Gas mark 3
Use a deep 20cm/8 inch round cake tin.

Combine the passion fruit juice, dried mixed fruit, orange juice, sugar and butter in saucepan. Stir constantly over the heat without boiling until the sugar dissolves. Bring to the boil, reduce heat, simmer uncovered for three minutes. Remove from heat; transfer to large bowl, cool to room temperature.

Grease the cake tin. Line the base and sides with paper. Stir the sour cream and sifted dry ingredients into cold fruit mixture. Pour into the prepared tin. Bake for about 1 ½ hours. Cover cake with foil, cool in the tin.

Lemon and Apricot Bread

FOR THE CAKE

METRIC	IMP.	US.	
175g	6 oz	1 ½ cups	white self-raising flour
100g	4 oz	½ cup	caster sugar
¼ tsp.	¼ tsp.	¼ tsp.	salt
100g	4 oz	½ cup	butter
4 tbs.	4 tbs.	4 tbs.	sour cream
125ml	8 tbs.	½ cup	milk
1 tbs.	1 tbs.	1 tbs.	grated lemon rind
1 tbs.	1 tbs.	1 tbs.	lemon juice
75g	3 oz	½ cup	sultanas
75g	3 oz	½ cup	chopped dried apricots

TOPPING.

METRIC	IMP.	US.	
100g	4 oz	½ cup	caster sugar
2 tbs.	2 tbs.	2 tbs.	lemon juice

Preheat the oven to 190°C/375°F/Gas mark 5
Use a 900g/2 lb loaf tin.

Grease the loaf tin. Melt the butter, and mix it in a bowl with the sugar. Add the sour cream and beat well. Add the sifted flour and salt, alternately with the milk. Mix well. Fold in the lemon rind, lemon juice, sultanas and apricots. Pour into the tin and level the surface. Bake for 50 to 60 minutes.

Topping: Stir the lemon juice and sugar in a saucepan over low heat until the sugar dissolves. While the teabread is still hot, spoon the topping over it. Allow to cool in the tin.

Orange Cranberry Bread (Vegan)

METRIC	IMP.	US.	
225g	8 oz	2 cups	white self-raising flour
½ tsp.	½ tsp.	½ tsp.	baking powder
½ tsp.	½ tsp.	½ tsp.	salt
100g	4 oz	½ cup	caster sugar
100g	4 oz	1 cup	chopped nuts
2 tbs.	2 tbs.	2 tbs.	vegetable margarine
175g	6 oz	1 cup	fresh or frozen cranberries
			juice and rind of one orange

Preheat the oven to 160°C/325°F/Gas mark 3
Use a 23cm/9 inch round cake tin.

Grease and line the cake tin. Add boiling water to the orange juice, rind and melted margarine to make ¾ cup. Sift together twice - flour, salt, baking powder and sugar. Add the juice and rind of the orange. Add the nuts and cranberries, mix all the ingredients, pour into the cake tin and bake for one hour, or until a warm knife inserted into the centre comes out clean. Leave to cool for 10 minutes, before placing on a wire rack to cool completely.

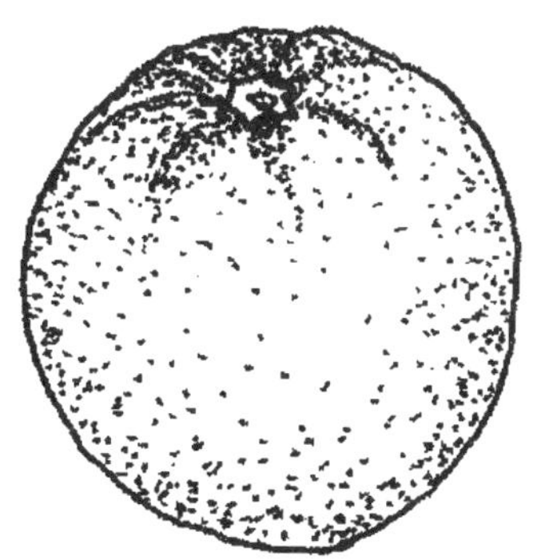

Orange and Sultana Cake (Vegan)

METRIC	IMP.	US.	
150g	5 oz	1 ¼ cups	white self-raising flour
150g	5 oz	1 ¼ cups	wholemeal self-raising flour
1 ½ tsp.	1 ½ tsp.	1 ½ tsp.	baking powder
175g	6 oz	¾ cup	light soft brown sugar
250ml	8 fl. oz	1 cup	soya milk
125ml	8 tbs.	½ cup	vegetable oil
1 tbs.	1 tbs.	1 tbs.	concentrated orange juice
175g	6 oz	1 cup	sultanas, washed and dried
			grated rind of ½ orange

Preheat the oven to 180°C/350°F/Gas mark 4
Use a 20cm/8 inch round cake tin.

Grease and line the cake tin. Sift the white flour and wholemeal flour into a large mixing bowl, adding any residue of bran left in the sieve. In another bowl, whisk together the oil, soya milk, orange juice and sugar. Make sure that the sugar has dissolved, then fold in the flour, sultanas and orange rind. Mix well, then spoon into the tin and level the surface.

Bake for about 1 hour, or until the cake feels firm to the touch and is beginning to shrink from the sides of the tin. Leave to firm up in the tin for 10 minutes, then turn out onto a wire tray, peel off the paper and allow to cool.

Lemon Almond Teabread

METRIC	IMP.	US.	
175g	6 oz	1 ½ cups	wholemeal self-raising flour
½ tsp.	½ tsp.	½ tsp.	baking powder
175g	6 oz	¾ cup	light brown soft sugar
2 tbs.	2 tbs.	2 tbs.	golden syrup
175g	6 oz	¾ cup	butter
6 tbs.	6 tbs.	6 tbs.	sour cream
½ tsp.	½ tsp.	½ tsp.	ground allspice
175g	6 oz	1 ½ cups	courgettes, coarsely grated
2 tbs.	2 tbs.	2 tbs.	fresh brown breadcrumbs
50g	2 oz	½ cup	flaked almonds
			finely grated rind of 1 lemon

Preheat the oven to 180°C/350°F/Gas mark 4
Use a 900g/2 lb loaf tin.

Grease the loaf tin and line with greaseproof paper. Cream the butter and sugar together until fluffy. Gradually beat in the sour cream. Fold in the flour, baking powder and allspice. Stir in the courgettes, grated lemon rind, breadcrumbs and most of the almonds. Spoon the mixture into the prepared tin.

Bake in the preheated oven for 50 minutes. Brush the teabread with golden syrup and sprinkle over the remaining almonds. Return to the oven and bake for a further 30 minutes or until well browned and firm to the touch. A warm knife inserted into the teabread should come out clean. Allow the teabread to cool slightly in the tin, then turn out on to a wire rack to cool completely.

Iced Lemon Sponge Cake

FOR THE CAKE

METRIC	IMP.	US.	
200g	7 oz	1 ¾ cups	white self-raising flour
50g	2 oz	½ cup	cornflour
½ tsp.	½ tsp.	½ tsp.	baking powder
100g	4 oz	½ cup	caster sugar
175g	6 oz	¾ cup	softened butter
4 tbs.	4 tbs.	4 tbs.	sour cream
125ml	8 tbs.	½ cup	milk
			grated rind of 1 lemon

SYRUP

METRIC	IMP.	US.	
2 tbs.	2 tbs.	2 tbs.	water
4 tbs.	4 tbs.	4 tbs.	sugar
1 tbs.	1 tbs.	1 tbs.	conc. apple juice
			juice of 1 lemon

LEMON ICING

METRIC	IMP.	US.	
100g	4 oz	1 cup	icing sugar
2 tbs.	2 tbs.	2 tbs.	lemon juice
			strip of lemon peel

Preheat the oven to 190°C/375°F/Gas mark 5
Use a 20cm/8 inch round cake tin.

Grease the cake tin and dust with flour. Beat together the butter, lemon rind and sugar until pale and creamy. Stir in the sour cream and milk then fold in the sifted flour, cornflour and baking powder. Turn into the prepared cake tin, smooth over the surface, and bake for 40-50 minutes. Turn on to a wire rack to cool.

Syrup and icing: Bring the water to the boil with the lemon juice and sugar. Add the concentrated apple juice and pour slowly over the cake, allowing the syrup to soak well in.

Mix the sifted icing sugar with the lemon juice until smooth and spread thickly on top of the cake, allowing it to fall over the sides. Shred the strip of lemon peel and sprinkle over the icing before it sets.

Orange Cherry Bread

METRIC	IMP.	US.	
275g	10 oz	2 ½ cups	white self-raising flour
1 tsp.	1 tsp.	1 tsp.	baking powder
¾ tsp.	¾ tsp.	¾ tsp.	salt
2 tbs.	2 tbs.	2 tbs.	melted butter
4 tbs.	4 tbs.	4 tbs.	sour cream
250ml	8 fl. oz	1 cup	milk
1 ½ tsp.	1 ½ tsp.	1 ½ tsp.	ground cinnamon
½ tsp.	½ tsp.	½ tsp.	ground nutmeg
175g	6 oz	¾ cup	sugar
100g	4 oz	½ cup	chopped glacé cherries
175g	6 oz	1 cup	chopped citron peel
2 tsp.	2 tsp.	2 tsp.	grated orange rind
			corn syrup for brushing

Preheat the oven to 180°C/350°F/Gas mark 4
Use a 900g/2 lb loaf tin.

Sift together the flour, baking powder, salt, spices and sugar. Stir in the fruit and grated orange rind until all is well coated with flour. Mix together the sour cream, milk and butter; stir into the dry ingredients until just blended. Pour into a the greased loaf tin and bake for 65 minutes. While bread is still hot, brush with hot corn syrup.

Carrot and Orange Cake (Vegan)

FOR THE CAKE

METRIC	IMP.	US.	
225g	8 oz	2 cups	white self-raising flour
½ tsp.	½ tsp.	½ tsp.	baking powder
6 tbs.	6 tbs.	6 tbs.	dark brown sugar
100g	4 oz	½ cup	soft vegetable margarine
100g	4 oz	1 cup	finely grated carrot
2 tsp.	2 tsp.	2 tsp.	ground cinnamon
125ml	8 tbs.	½ cup	soya milk
			grated rind of 1 orange

TOPPING

METRIC	IMP.	US.	
50g	2 oz	½ cup	creamed coconut
			juice of 1 orange

Preheat the oven to 180°C/350°F/Gas mark 4
Use a 15cm/6 inch cake tin.

Grease and line the tin. Cream the margarine with the sugar until light and fluffy. Stir in the carrot and orange rind. Fold in the flour, baking powder and cinnamon. Add milk and mix well. Transfer the mixture to the greased cake tin with a circle of greaseproof paper in the base. Bake for 1 hour in the preheated oven. Remove the cake from the tin and set it to cool on a wire rack. Meanwhile, melt the coconut over a low heat. Stir in the orange juice and spread the mixture evenly over the cake.

Lemon Yoghurt Sponge Cake

FOR THE CAKE

METRIC	IMP.	US.	
225g	8 oz	2 cups	white self raising flour, sifted
1	1	1	pinch salt
100g.	4 oz.	½ cup	caster sugar
4 tbs.	4 tbs.	4 tbs.	butter
125ml	8 tbs.	½ cup	plain yoghurt
			grated rind of 1 small lemon

ICING AND DECORATION

METRIC	IMP.	US.	
150g	5 oz	1 ¼ cup	icing sugar, sifted
2 tbs.	2 tbs.	2 tbs.	fresh lemon juice
1 tsp.	1 tsp.	1 tsp.	caster sugar
			finely pared rind of ½ lemon

Preheat the oven to 180°C/350°F/Gas mark 4
Use a 20cm/8 inch round cake tin.

Grease and base line the tin. Sift together the flour and salt. Add the butter, caster sugar, yoghurt and lemon rind and beat until smooth and thick. Spoon the mixture into the tin and level the surface. Bake for about 1¼ hours, or until the cake is risen, firm to the touch and shrinking from the sides of the tin. Allow to firm up in the tin for 5 minutes, then turn out onto a wire tray.

Icing and decoration: Pour the lemon juice into the icing sugar to achieve a spreadable icing. Take care not to add too much juice as it is very easy to make the icing too thin. Spread the icing on the cooled cake. Cut the pared rind into the thinnest strips you can. Put the strips into a small pan with water just to cover. Bring to the boil and drain, then cover with fresh water. Stir in the sugar and boil for 1 - 2 minutes until the peel is soft. Drain the peel in a sieve and cool under the cold tap. Pat it dry on kitchen paper and scatter on top of the icing.

THE SACRED WATERS OF LETCHMORE HEATH.

CAKES WITH COCONUT.

Bhaktivedanta Manor is situated just to the north of London, in the green belt around the City. A great many Hindus live in the north and west of the metropolis, and since 1973 many have made the Manor their spiritual home. In the picturesque village of Letchmore Heath, where property prices are sky-high, the influx of visitors has been opposed by an influential minority, who have tried for many years to prevent visitors coming to pray.

As well as *darshan* at the shrine of the presiding deities, Sri-Sri Radha Gokulananda, the temple offers classes in the scriptures, a Sunday school, the youth forum and a spiritual atmosphere in general. Sunday afternoon is a popular time for families, especially in the summer, when they can walk around the lake, picnic on the lawn and feed the cows.

The Manor offers a more unusual facility for the Hindu community. Coconuts, as bananas, are an important part of ceremonies. They are placed at the four corners of the altar and after the service is over, they are considered sacred. Traditionally, remnants from such observances should be placed into the Ganges, or a local holy river. Britain is sadly lacking in such bodies of water, and, since 1973, it has fallen to the boating lake at the Manor to take on this important role.

In 1991, the lake was drained and hundreds of coconuts, flower garlands and even broken family deities were found. After dredging, and a refill, the lake is again playing this important role. On any day, you can follow the Bhagavad Gita walk around the shore and see the dark brown shapes bobbing up and down between the ducks and the newly planted water lilies.

Bhagavat

Coconut and Caramel C

FOR THE CAKE

METRIC	IMP.	US.	
175g	6 oz	1 ½ cups	white self-raising flour
4 tbs.	4 tbs.	4 tbs.	brown sugar, firmly packed
50g	2 oz	½ cup	dessicated coconut
100g	4 oz	½ cup	butter
4 tbs.	4 tbs.	4 tbs.	sour cream
2 tbs.	2 tbs.	2 tbs.	golden syrup
125ml	8 tbs.	½ cup	milk

CARAMEL ICING

METRIC	IMP.	US.	
175g	6 oz	1 ½ cups	icing sugar
6 tbs.	6 tbs.	6 tbs.	butter
100g	4 oz	½ cup	brown sugar
2 tbs.	2 tbs.	2 tbs.	milk

Preheat the oven to 180°C/350°F/Gas mark 4
Use a 19cm x 29cm lamington tin.

Line the base of the lamington tin with greaseproof paper. Grease the paper. Stir coconut constantly over heat in heavy frying pan until light golden brown. Remove from pan to cool. Cream the butter and sugar in small bowl until light and fluffy, add the sour cream and golden syrup and mix well. Transfer the mixture to large bowl, stir in the toasted coconut, half the sifted flour and half the milk, then stir in remaining flour and milk. Spread mixture into prepared tin.

Bake in the preheated oven for about 35 minutes. Allow to stand for 5 minutes before turning on to wire rack to cool. Spread the cold cake with icing, sprinkling with extra coconut if desired.

Caramel Icing. Melt butter in saucepan, add sugar, stir constantly over heat without boiling for about 2 minutes. Stir in milk then gradually stir in sifted icing sugar, stir until smooth.

Toasted Coconut Cake

METRIC	IMP.	US.	
350g	12 oz	3 cups	white self-raising flour
175g	6 oz	¾ cup	brown sugar
1 tsp.	1 tsp.	1 tsp.	baking powder
1 tsp.	1 tsp.	1 tsp.	salt
100g	4 oz	1 cup	dessicated coconut
2 tsp.	2 tsp.	2 tsp.	grated orange peel
2 tbs.	2 tbs.	2 tbs.	sour cream
450ml	¾ pint	1 ¾ cups	milk
175g	6 oz	¾ cup	butter
1 tsp.	1 tsp.	1 tsp.	vanilla essence

Preheat the oven to 180°C/350°F/Gas mark 4
Use a 900g/2 lb loaf tin.

Grease and line the loaf tin. Cream together the sugar and butter. Sift in the self-raising flour, baking powder and salt. Stir in the sugar, coconut and peel. Combine the remaining ingredients and add to the dry mixture all at once. Stir until well mixed. Turn the batter into the greased loaf tin. Bake for 60 to 70 minutes. Allow to cool for 10 minutes and remove from the tin. Place on a wire rack to cool completely.

Caribbean Cake

METRIC	IMP.	US	
225g	8 oz	2 cups	white flour
1 tsp.	1 tsp.	1 tsp.	bicarb
¼ tbs.	¼ tbs.	¼ tbs.	salt
½ tsp.	½ tsp.	½ tsp.	ground allspice.
50g	2 oz	¼ cup	melted butter
125ml	4 fl. oz	½ cup	coconut milk
125ml	4 fl. oz	½ cup	sweetened condensed milk.

Preheat the oven to 180°C/350°F/Gas mark 4.
Use a 23cm/9 inch round cake tin.

Grease and line the tin. Sift together the flour, salt, bicarb and allspice. Work in the melted butter. Pour in the sweetened condensed milk and coconut milk. Mix well.

Spoon into the prepared tin and bake in the oven for 40 minutes, or until a warm knife inserted into the centre comes out clean. Allow to cool in the tin for 15 minutes and turn out onto a wire rack.

Kentish Coconut Cake

METRIC	IMP.	US.	
225g	8 oz	2 cups	white self-raising white flour
100g	4 oz	½ cup	butter
100g	4 oz	½ cup	caster sugar
300ml	½ pint	1 ¼ cups	sour cream
3 tbs.	3 tbs.	3 tbs.	carob powder
50g	2 oz	½ cup	desiccated coconut
3 tbs.	3 tbs.	3 tbs.	ground almonds
1 tbs.	1 tbs.	1 tbs.	golden syrup, warmed
¼ tsp.	¼ tsp.	¼ tsp.	vanilla essence

Preheat the oven to 190°C/375°F/Gas mark 5
Use a 15cm/6 inch cake tin.

Grease and line the tin. Cream butter and sugar until light. Beat in the sour cream. Sift the flour and carob and mix in the coconut and almonds. Fold the sifted ingredients into the creamed mixture with the golden syrup. Add the vanilla. Turn the mixture into the tin. Bake in the centre of the oven for 50 minutes or until a warm knife inserted comes out clean. Allow to shrink slightly before turning out on to a wire tray to cool.

Coconut Orange Cake

FOR THE CAKE

METRIC	IMP.	US.	
200g	7 oz	1 ¾ cups	white self-raising flour
½ tsp.	½ tsp.	½ tsp.	baking powder
100g	4 oz	½ cup	caster sugar
100g	4 oz	½ cup	butter
300ml	½ pint	1 ¼ cups	milk
1 tbs.	1 tbs.	1 tbs.	grated orange rind
50g	2 oz	½ cup	dessicated coconut
4 tbs.	4 tbs.	4 tbs.	sour cream

ORANGE ICING

METRIC	IMP.	US.	
225g	8 oz	2 cups	icing sugar
2 tbs.	2 tbs.	2 tbs.	soft butter
2 tbs.	2 tbs.	2 tbs.	orange juice, approximately

Preheat the oven to 160°C/325°F/Gas mark 3
Use a 900g/2 lb loaf tin.

Combine the coconut and milk and stand at room temperature for 1 hour. Grease and line the loaf tin. Cream the butter, rind and sugar in small bowl until light and fluffy; stir in the sour cream and mix well. Transfer this mixture to a large bowl and stir in half the coconut mixture with half the sifted flour and the baking powder. Then stir in the remaining coconut mixture and flour. Stir until smooth. Pour mixture into the prepared tin.

Bake for about 1 ½ hours. Allow to stand for 10 minutes, before turning on to wire rack to cool. Spread cold cake with icing; decorate with orange wedges if desired.

Orange Icing: Sift icing sugar into bowl, stir in butter and enough juice to mix to a spreadable consistency.

Coconut and Cherry Cake

Wash any excess syrup from glacé cherries before use and dry thoroughly, then toss in a little flour. This will avoid the cherries sinking to the bottom during cooking.

METRIC	IMP.	US.	
225g	8 oz	2 cups	white self-raising flour
½ tsp.	½ tsp.	½ tsp.	baking powder
100g	4 oz	½ cup	soft brown sugar
100g	4 oz	1 cup	desiccated coconut
¼ tsp.	¼ tsp.	¼ tsp.	salt
175g	6 oz	¾ cup	butter or margarine
250ml	8 fl. oz	1 cup	milk
100g	4 oz	½ cup	glacé cherries - chopped fine
4 tbs.	4 tbs.	4 tbs.	sour cream

Preheat the oven to 180°C/350°F/Gas mark 4
Use a 900g/2 lb loaf tin.

Line the base of the loaf tin with greaseproof paper, grease the paper and dust with flour. Put the flour and salt into a bowl and rub in the butter until the mixture resembles fine breadcrumbs. Stir in the desiccated coconut, sugar and cherries. Reserve 2 tbs. of the coconut. Whisk together the sour cream and milk and beat into the dry ingredients. Turn the mixture into the tin and level the surface. Scatter the desiccated coconut over the top.

Bake for 1 ½ hours. Test with a warm knife. Check after 40 minutes and cover with greaseproof paper if overbrowning. Turn out on to a wire rack to cool.

Coconut Pineapple Cake

FOR THE CAKE

METRIC	IMP.	US.	
225g	8 oz	2 cups	white self-raising flour
175g	6 oz	¾ cup	caster sugar
100g	4 oz	½ cup	butter
2 tsp.	2 tsp.	2 tsp.	grated lemon rind
4 tbs.	4 tbs.	4 tbs.	sour cream
50g	2 oz	½ cup	desiccated coconut
300ml	½ pint	1 ¼ cups	pineapple juice

PINEAPPLE ICING

METRIC	IMP.	US.	
275g	10 oz	2 ½ cups	icing sugar
2 tbs.	2 tbs.	2 tbs.	butter
5 tbs.	5 tbs.	5 tbs.	pineapple juice

Preheat the oven to 160°C/325°F/Gas mark 3
Use a deep 20cm/8 inch round cake tin.

Line the base of the cake tin with greaseproof paper and grease the paper. Cream the butter, rind and sugar in small bowl until light and fluffy. Add the sour cream and mix well. Transfer mixture to large bowl, stir in the coconut, then half the sifted flour and pineapple juice. Add the remaining flour and pineapple juice; stir until combined. Spread the mixture into the prepared tin.
Bake for about 1 hour. Allow to stand 10 minutes before turning on to wire rack to cool. When cold, spread with icing. Decorate with extra pineapple and coconut if desired.

Pineapple Icing: Combine butter and sifted icing sugar in bowl, gradually stir in pineapple juice until smooth.

GATHERING THE AUTUMN HARVEST

CAKES WITH FRESH FRUIT.

In 1989 I was asked to take part in a multi-faith pilgrimage to Canterbury Cathedral. I had just arrived in England from South Africa, and the idea was an attractive one. The pilgrimage, on the theme of 'Faith and the Environment', was organised by Ranchor Prime, a Hare Krishna devotee and consultant for the WWF. I was staying at the vibrant Hare Krishna temple in London's Soho Street, but the starting point was out at Bhaktivedanta Manor.

Our small group, composed of members of seven different faiths, set out across the fields from the Manor on a warm September morning. My first impression of the English countryside was the abundance of Autumn berries, so different from anything in my Natal home. I was surprised to see so much fruit neglected on the branches. I sampled some of the tasty berries and wondered at the Britisher's lack of interest in their natural produce.

The walk took us first into central London. Each night we rested at different places of worship. One night we would stay in a Synagogue, another in a Gurdhwara. We met with Christians, Hindus and Buddhists. Soon we passed out of town into the fields of Kent. Our path took us through some of the largest orchards in the country. I was shocked by the extensive neglect. Thousands of ripe apples lay spoiled on the ground. Mile upon mile of fruit trees were left to rot.

My mind went back to childhood days in my grandmothers orchard just north of Durban. She cultivated mangoes, litchis, bananas, pineapples, peaches, lemons and avocados. She was after us with a stick if she caught us on a childhood foray. She forbade any waste of the produce of the land, and was a perfect example of the Vaishnava motto 'Simple living and high thinking'.

We stood in Kent in the midst of ruin. I never did not find out the reason for such sinful neglect. I can only imagine that 'market forces' were a factor. Perhaps Australian or New Zealand apples filled the shelves of the local supermarket. The experience had a deep and lasting effect on me.

Now, when autumn comes, we are fully prepared to deal with the harvest. My husband has a knack of finding neglected fruit trees. Our favourite spot is a small unstaffed railway station to the west of Watford, which operates for only three trains each day. Alongside the platform grow the most enormous blackberries. There are loganberries and raspberries on the embankment, pears and apples on the trackside. The real bounty however is the dozen or so plum trees, planted by a station-master in days gone bye. Now we pick them to make chutney for Radharani, Krishna's consort, whose celebration day falls in September.

Akinchana.

Sultana Apple Cake

METRIC	IMP.	US.	
350g	12 oz	3 cups	white self-raising flour
1 tsp.	1 tsp.	1 tsp.	baking powder
175g	6 oz	¾ cup	light soft brown
250g	9 oz	1 ½ cups	sultanas
225g	8 oz	1 ½ cups	cooking apples
125ml	8 tbs.	½ cup	milk
2 tsp.	2 tsp.	2 tsp.	ground mixed spice
175g	6 oz	¾ cup	butter, melted
2 tbs.	2 tbs.	2 tbs.	sour cream
4 tbs.	4 tbs.	4 tbs.	demerara sugar for sprinkling
			finely grated rind of 1 lemon

Preheat the oven to 160°C/325°F/Gas mark 3
Use a 20cm/8 inch square cake tin.

Grease and line the cake tin. Peel, core and chop the apples. Mix the sultanas, apples and milk and set aside. Sift the sugar, flour and spice and stir in the lemon rind. Gradually beat in the butter and sour cream. Finally beat in the apple mixture. Turn into the prepared tin.

Sprinkle the demerara sugar over the top and bake in the preheated oven for 1 ½ - 1 ¾ hours until well risen and firm to the touch. Cool slightly before turning out onto a rack.

Fresh Apple Nut Bread

METRIC	IMP.	US.	
350g	12 oz	3 cups	white self-raising flour
1 tsp.	1 tsp.	1 tsp.	baking powder
6 tbs.	6 tbs.	6 tbs.	butter
175g	6 oz	¾ cup	packed light brown sugar
4 tbs.	4 tbs.	4 tbs.	sour cream
1 tsp.	1 tsp.	1 tsp.	salt
½ tsp.	½ tsp.	½ tsp.	grated fresh lemon rind
75g	3 oz	¾ cup	chopped nuts
1 tsp.	1 tsp.	1 tsp.	cinnamon
¼ tsp.	¼ tsp.	¼ tsp.	nutmeg
100g	4 oz	1 cup	grated apple (1 large)
300ml	½ pint	1 ¼ cups	buttermilk

Preheat the oven to 180°C/350°F/Gas mark 4
Use a 900g/2 lb loaf tin.

Grease and line the cake tin. In a medium bowl cream together the butter and sugar, beat in the sour cream. Mix the flour, baking powder, salt, lemon rind, nuts, cinnamon, nutmeg and grated apple. Blend into the creamed mixture, alternately with buttermilk. Turn into the loaf tin and bake for one hour. Cool for 10 minutes. Remove from tin and cool on a wire rack. Makes one loaf.

Spiced Apple Cake

FOR THE CAKE

METRIC	IMP.	US.	
350g	12 oz	3 cups	white self-raising flour
175g	6 oz	¾ cup	caster sugar
1 tsp.	1 tsp.	1 tsp.	baking powder
175g	6 oz	¾ cup	butter
4 tbs.	4 tbs.	4 tbs.	sour cream
1 tsp.	1 tsp.	1 tsp.	salt
1 tsp.	1 tsp.	1 tsp.	ground cinnamon
300ml	½ pint	1 ¼ cups	milk
225g	8 oz	1 ¾ cups	chopped apples

TOPPING

METRIC	IMP.	US.	
225g	8 oz	1 cup	brown sugar
75g	3 oz	¾ cup	finely chopped mixed nuts
½ tsp.	½ tsp.	½ tsp.	ground cinnamon

Preheat the oven to 180°C/350°F/Gas mark 4
Use a 14 inch cake tin.

Grease and line the cake tin. Cream together the butter and the sugar. Beat in the sour cream and blend well. Sift together the flour, baking powder, salt and a teaspoon of cinnamon. Add to the creamed mixture, alternately with milk. Fold in the apples. Pour into the cake tin.

Topping: Combine the brown sugar, nuts and ½ tsp. cinnamon. Sprinkle over the batter. Bake for about 30 minutes. Test with a warm knife. Allow to cool for 10 minutes before removing to cool completely on a wire rack.

Apple Spice Loaf

FOR THE CAKE

METRIC	IMP.	US.	
350g	12 oz	3 cups	wholemeal self-raising flour
2 tsp.	2 tsp.	2 tsp.	baking powder
¼ tsp.	¼ tsp.	¼ tsp.	ground mace
1 tsp.	1 tsp.	1 tsp.	ground nutmeg
1 tsp.	1 tsp.	1 tsp.	ground cinnamon
¼ tsp.	¼ tsp.	¼ tsp.	ground cloves
175g	6 oz	¾ cup	butter
175g	6 oz	¾ cup	soft brown sugar
450g	1 lb	2 ½ cups	cooking apples
4 tbs.	4 tbs.	4 tbs.	water
2 tbs.	2 tbs.	2 tbs.	lemon juice
100g	4 oz	1 cup	walnuts chopped
75g	3 oz	½ cup	sultanas
175g	6 oz	1 cup	chopped dates
3 tbs.	3 tbs.	3 tbs.	milk

TOPPING:

METRIC	IMP.	US.	
1 tbs.	1 tbs.	1 tbs.	demerara sugar
25g	1 oz	¼ cup	chopped walnuts
½ tsp.	½ tsp.	½ tsp.	cinnamon

Preheat the oven to 160°C/325°F/Gas mark 3
Use a 900g/2 lb loaf tin.

Grease and line the loaf tin. Peel and core the apples and place with lemon juice and water in a saucepan. Cook over a low heat until the fruit is soft and pulpy. Mash with a wooden spoon and leave to cool. Place the butter and sugar in a large mixing bowl and beat until light and fluffy. Add flour to the bowl and sift the baking powder, cloves, cinnamon, nutmeg and mace over the top.

Add the apple mixture, walnuts, sultanas, dates and stir until all the ingredients are evenly mixed with the creamed mixture. Stir in the milk. Spoon the mixture into the prepared tin and smooth the surface.

Topping: Mix the sugar, nuts and cinnamon together and sprinkle over the uncooked cake. Bake for 1 ¼ to 1 ½ hours. Test with a warm knife. Allow to cool in the baking tin for 15 minutes then invert onto wire rack to cool completely.

Dorset Apple Cake

FOR THE CAKE

METRIC	IMP.	US.	
175g	6 oz	1 ½ cups	white self raising flour
100g	4 oz	½ cup	brown sugar
2	2	2	large cooking apples
4 tbs.	4 tbs.	4 tbs.	butter
75g	3 oz	½ cup	currants
2 tbs.	2 tbs.	2 tbs.	sour cream
Extra	Extra	Extra	butter, sugar for sprinkling

Preheat the oven to 180°C/350°F/Gas mark 4
Use a 20cm/8 inch square cake tin.

Grease and line the cake tin. Peel, core and finely chop the apples. Rub the butter into the flour. Stir in the chopped apples, brown sugar and currants. Gradually incorporate the sour cream and make a smooth dough. Turn it into the prepared cake tin and bake for ¾ hour or until a warm knife inserted into the cake comes out clean.

Turn the cake out onto a warm dish, split it horizontally and butter the lower layer. Sprinkle it generously with brown sugar, replace the top and sprinkle with caster sugar. Serve immediately.

Apple and Cinnamon Cake

METRIC	IMP.	US.	
275g	10 oz	2 ½ cups	white self-raising flour
1 ½ tsp.	1 ½ tsp.	1 ½ tsp.	baking powder
100g	4 oz	½ cup	demerara sugar
100g	4 oz	½ cup	butter, melted
225g	8 oz	1 ½ cups	apples
1 ½ tsp.	1 ½ tsp.	1 ½ tsp.	ground cinnamon
½ tsp.	½ tsp.	½ tsp.	salt
75g	3 oz	½ cup	raisins
2 tbs.	2 tbs.	2 tbs.	sour cream
125ml	8 tbs.	½ cup	milk
			icing sugar for dredging

Preheat the oven to 180°C/350°F/Gas mark 4
Use a 23cm/9 inch round cake tin.

Grease and line the cake tin. Peel, core and chop the apples. Sift the flour, cinnamon and salt into a bowl and stir in the sugar and raisins. Mix in the butter, sour cream, milk and apples and beat until smooth. Turn the mixture into the prepared baking tin and bake for 1 to 1 ¼ hrs. Test with a warm knife before turning out onto a wire rack to cool. Sprinkle with icing sugar.

Apple, Cheese and Nut Loaf

METRIC	IMP.	US.	
225g	8 oz	2 cups	wholemeal self-raising flour
1 tsp.	1 tsp.	1 tsp.	baking powder
1 tsp.	1 tsp.	1 tsp.	cinnamon
½ tsp.	½ tsp.	½ tsp.	salt
100g	4 oz	½ cup	brown sugar
100g	4 oz	1 cup	grated veg. Cheddar cheese
50g	2 oz	½ cup	chopped walnuts
2	2	2	apples, peeled and chopped
2 tbs.	2 tbs.	2 tbs.	sour cream
6 tbs.	6 tbs.	6 tbs.	melted butter
1 tbs.	1 tbs.	1 tbs.	milk

Preheat the oven to 180°C/350°F/Gas mark 4
Use a 900g/2 lb loaf tin.

Grease and line the loaf tin. Sift together the flour, baking powder, cinnamon and salt. Add the sugar, grated cheese, walnuts and apples and mix well. Whisk together the butter, milk and sour cream and add to the dry ingredients. Mix thoroughly. Turn the mixture into the loaf tin and bake for 1 hour. Test with a warm knife. Allow to stand for 10 minutes. Remove and turn out onto a wire rack to cool.

Apple Sauce Cake (Vegan)

METRIC	IMP.	US.	
225g	8 oz	2 cups	white self-raising flour
½ tsp.	½ tsp.	½ tsp.	baking powder
100g	4 oz	½ cup	vegetable margarine
½ tsp.	½ tsp.	½ tsp.	salt
100g	4 oz	½ cup	soft brown sugar
75g	3 oz	½ cup	raisins
75g	3 oz	½ cup	stoned chopped dates
½ tsp.	½ tsp.	½ tsp.	ground cinnamon
½ tsp.	½ tsp.	½ tsp.	ground cloves
½ tsp.	½ tsp.	½ tsp.	ground allspice
½ tsp.	½ tsp.	½ tsp.	ground nutmeg
225g	8 oz	1 ½ cups	unsweetened apple puree
2 tbs.	2 tbs.	2 tbs.	soya milk
50g	2 oz	½ cup	chopped walnuts

Preheat the oven to 180°C/350°F/Gas mark 4
Use a 23cm/9 inch square cake tin.

Grease and line the cake tin. Put the raisins, dates, spices and 8 tbs. water in a saucepan. Boil rapidly, then strain and leave to cool. Sift the flour, baking powder and salt together. Add the sugar, margarine and apple puree. Mix well and add all other remaining ingredients. Pour the mixture into the baking tin and bake for 50-60 minutes. Test with a warm knife before turning out onto a wire rack to cool. This cake keeps very well.

Parisian Apple Gingerbread

METRIC	IMP.	US.	
225g	8 oz	2 cups	white self-raising flour
1 tsp.	1 tsp.	1 tsp.	baking powder
100g	4 oz	½ cup	unsweetened apple puree
6 tbs.	6 tbs.	6 tbs.	dark brown sugar
75g	3 oz	¼ cup	golden syrup
6 tbs.	6 tbs.	6 tbs.	butter
1 tsp.	1 tsp.	1 tsp.	ground ginger
75g	3 oz	½ cup	raisins
1 tsp.	1 tsp.	1 tsp.	caraway seeds
2 tsp.	2 tsp.	2 tsp.	sour cream
1 tsp.	1 tsp.	1 tsp.	lemon juice

Preheat the oven to 180°C/350°F/Gas mark 4
Use a 900g/2 lb loaf tin.

Grease and line the loaf tin. Sift the flour with ginger, stir in the raisins and caraway seeds. Mix in the sour cream with the lemon juice and add the apple puree along with the melted butter, sugar and golden syrup. Beat well until smooth and pour into the loaf tin. Bake for an hour. After removing from oven allow to cool for 30 minutes before turning out.

Dutch Apple Tea-Bread

METRIC	IMP.	US.	
225g	8 oz	2 cups	white self-raising flour
½ tsp.	½ tsp.	½ tsp.	baking powder
100g	4 oz	½ cup	butter
100g	4 oz	½ cup	brown sugar
2 tbs.	2 tbs.	2 tbs.	sour cream
1 tsp.	1 tsp.	1 tsp.	vanilla essence
1 tsp.	1 tsp.	1 tsp.	bicarb.
½ tsp.	½ tsp.	½ tsp.	salt
125ml	8 tbs.	½ cup	orange juice
225g	8 oz	1 ½ cups	cooking apples diced

Preheat the oven to 180°C/350°F/Gas mark 4
Use a 900g/2 lb loaf tin.

Grease and line the loaf tin. Cream the butter and sugar. Stir in sour cream and vanilla essence. Sift the dry ingredients and fold in with the orange juice. Fold in the apples and turn the mixture into the loaf tin. Bake for 55 mins. Cool in the tin and turn out onto a wire rack.

Danish Apple Cake

METRIC	IMP.	US.	
200g	7 oz	1 ¾ cups	white self-raising flour
½ tsp.	½ tsp.	½ tsp.	baking powder
100g	4 oz	½ cup	butter
175g	6 oz	¾ cup	caster sugar
2 tbs.	2 tbs.	2 tbs.	sour cream
125ml	8 tbs.	½ cup	milk
3	3	3	dessert apples
½ tsp.	½ tsp.	½ tsp.	cinnamon
			extra sugar for sprinkling

Preheat the oven to 180°C/350°F/Gas mark 4
Use a 23cm/9 inch loose bottom cake tin.

Grease and line the cake tin. Cream together the butter and sugar. Gradually add the sour cream. Sift together the flour and baking powder and fold into the mixture, alternating with the milk. Peel, core and finely slice the apples. Turn half the mixture into the greased baking tin and cover with half the apples. Add the remaining mixture and arrange the rest of the apples on top. Sprinkle with cinnamon and sugar and bake for 55 minutes.

Blackcurrant Tea Bread

METRIC	IMP.	US.	
225g	8 oz	2 cups	self-raising flour
1 tsp.	1 tsp.	1tsp.	ground cinnamon
100g	4 oz	½ cup	butter
100g	4 oz	½ cup	soft brown sugar
pinch	pinch	pinch	salt
			grated rind of 1 lemon
2 tbs.	2 tbs.	2 tbs.	lemon juice
175g	6 oz	1 cup	fresh blackcurrants
4 tbs.	4 tbs.	4 tbs.	sour cream
			a little sugar for sprinkling

Preheat the oven to 180°C/350°F/Gas Mark 4.
Use a 900g/2 lb loaf tin.

Grease and line the loaf tin. Sieve the flour and cinnamon together, rub in the butter, then fold in the sugar, salt, lemon rind and juice, blackcurrants and sour cream. Mix thoroughly. Spoon into the prepared cake tin. Sprinkle the extra sugar over the top and push down any visible blackcurrants.

Bake for 50-60 minutes in the preheated oven. Check to see if a warm knife inserted in the centre comes out clean. Cool in the tin for 10 minutes and remove to a wire rack to cool completely.

Apple Buttermilk Cake

FOR THE CAKE

METRIC	IMP.	US.	
100g	4 oz	1 cup	white self-raising white flour
100g	4 oz	1 cup	wholemeal self-raising flour
100g	4 oz	½ cup	butter
1 tsp.	1 tsp.	1 tsp.	baking powder
100g	4 oz	1 cup	sugar
1 tsp.	1 tsp.	1 tsp.	sour cream
300ml	½ pint	1 ¼ cups	buttermilk
1 tsp.	1 tsp.	1 tsp.	salt
2	2	2	dessert apples cored and sliced
1 tsp.	1 tsp.	1 tsp.	cinnamon

TOPPING:

METRIC	IMP.	US.	
1 tbs.	1 tbs.	1 tbs.	brown sugar
½ tsp.	½ tsp.	½ tsp.	cinnamon

Preheat the oven to 200°C/400°F/Gas mark 6
Use two 18cm/7 inch cake tins.

Grease and line the cake tins. Cream together the butter and sugar, add sour cream. Sift the remaining ingredients and fold in. Include any bran that remains in the sieve. Pour the mixture into the cake tins, level out. Spread the topping ingredients over one of the cakes. Bake for 10 minutes, and then lower the heat to 180C/350F/gas mark 4. Bake for a further 30 minutes. When cool sandwich the cakes together with jam or butter cream.

Kurdish Apple Cake.

This is a particular favourite of the Kurds of the Dierbekir region in Turkey where some of the world's most beautiful and delicious apples are grown. Serve warm or cold.

METRIC	IMP.	US.	
275g	10 oz	2 ½ cups	white self raising flour
1 ½ tsp.	1 ½ tsp.	1 ½ tsp.	baking powder
225g	8 oz	1 cup	unsalted butter
175g	6 oz	¾ cup	caster sugar
2 tbs.	2 tbs.	2 tbs.	sour cream
6	6	6	medium cooking apples
1 tsp.	1 tsp.	1 tsp.	ground cinnamon
4 tbs.	4 tbs.	4 tbs.	icing sugar
			double cream to serve

Preheat the oven to 180°C/350°F/Gas mark 4
Use a 12 x 9 inch/30 x 22.5 cm cake tin.

Line and grease the cake tin. Peel, core and slice the apples. Cream the butter and caster sugar in a large bowl until light and fluffy. Add the sour cream and beat until smooth. Sift in the flour and baking powder and work until the mixture becomes a soft, smooth dough. Divide the dough into 2 equal parts.

Roll out each ball of dough on a lightly floured work top to the approximate size of the cake tin. Lay one layer of the dough into the bottom of the tin and press down gently. Arrange the apple slices over the dough and sprinkle evenly with the cinnamon and the icing sugar. Cover with the other sheet of dough and press the edges down gently. Bake for 25-30 minutes or until a light golden colour, Remove from the oven. Serve warm or cold cut into 5 cm (2 inch) squares.

Gooseberry Cake

METRIC	IMP.	US.	
225g	8 oz	2 cups	white self-raising flour
1 tsp.	1 tsp.	1 tsp.	baking powder
100g	4 oz	½ cup	light muscovado sugar
100g	4 oz	½ cup	melted butter
6 tbs.	6 tbs.	6 tbs.	sour cream
6 tbs.	6 tbs.	6 tbs.	milk
350g	12 oz	3 cups	gooseberries, topped and tailed
1 tbs.	1 tbs.	1 tbs.	Demerara sugar for topping
			grated rind of 1 lemon

Preheat the oven to 180°C/350°F/Gas mark 4
Use a 20cm/8 inch loose-bottomed round cake tin.

Grease and line the cake tin. Measure all the ingredients, except the gooseberries, into a bowl and beat well until thoroughly blended. Spoon half of the mixture into the tin and level out. Top with the gooseberries, and then roughly spoon over the remaining mixture.

Bake in the oven for about 1 hour 20 minutes, until golden brown and shrinking away from the sides of the tin slightly. Allow to cool for 15 minutes then remove from the tin and serve warm with cream.

Apple Molasses Cake (Vegan)

METRIC	IMP.	US.	
275g	10 oz	2 ½ cups	wholemeal self-raising flour
1 ½ tsp.	1 ½ tsp.	1 ½ tsp.	baking powder
175g	6 oz	1 cup	thinly sliced apple
175g	6 oz	½ cup	golden syrup
2 tbs.	2 tbs.	2 tbs.	molasses
125ml	8 tbs.	½ cup	hot water
100g	4 oz	½ cup	brown sugar
1 tsp.	1 tsp.	1 tsp.	ground cinnamon
½ tsp.	½ tsp.	½ tsp.	ground cloves
¼ tsp.	¼ tsp.	¼ tsp.	grated nutmeg
¼ tsp.	¼ tsp.	¼ tsp.	salt (optional)
6 tbs.	6 tbs.	6 tbs.	vegetable margarine

Preheat the oven to 180°C/350°F/Gas mark 4
Use a 23cm/9 inch round cake tin.

Grease and line the cake tin. Mix the syrup and molasses. Fold in the apples and cook on a low flame until they are tender. Allow to cool. Melt the margarine in the hot water and mix the liquid gradually into the flour. Add all the other dry ingredients, little by little, constantly stirring to keep smooth. Finally stir in the syrup-apple-molasses mixture. Pour into the tin and bake 45-60 minutes. Test with a warm knife. Allow to cool in the tin before turning out.

Fresh Pear and Bran Cake

METRIC	IMP.	US.	
150g	5 oz	1 ¼ cups	white self-raising flour
½ tsp.	½ tsp.	½ tsp.	baking powder
50g	2 oz	½ cup	finely chopped walnuts
100g	4 oz	½ cup	demarara sugar
1 tsp.	1 tsp.	1 tsp.	ground cinnamon
2 tsp.	2 tsp.	2 tsp.	wheat bran
175g	6 oz	1 cup	thinly sliced pear
½ tsp.	½ tsp.	½ tsp.	lemon juice
175g	6 oz	¾ cup	butter
125ml	8 tbs.	½ cup	sour cream
½ tsp.	½ tsp.	½ tsp.	milk

Preheat the oven to 180°C/350°F/Gas mark 4
Use a 900g/2 lb loaf tin.

Grease and line the loaf tin. In a bowl, combine the walnuts, a third of the sugar, cinnamon, bran, pear slices and lemon juice. In a large bowl, cream together the butter and remaining sugar. Beat in the sour cream and milk.

Sift together the flour and baking powder and stir into the butter-sugar-sour cream mixture. Pour half of this batter into the tin. Spread the fruit and nut mixture over this, then spread the rest of the batter. Bake for 50 minutes. Stand in the tin for ten minutes, and turn out onto a wire rack to cool.

Blueberry Loaf

METRIC	IMP.	US.	
275g	10 oz	2 ½ cups	white self-raising flour
1 tsp.	1 tsp.	1 tsp.	baking powder
6 tbs.	6 tbs.	6 tbs.	butter
225g	8 oz	1 cup	brown sugar
2 tbs.	2 tbs.	2 tbs.	sour cream
1 tbs.	1 tbs.	1 tbs.	grated orange rind
125ml	8 tbs.	½ cup	milk
5 tbs.	5 tbs.	5 tbs.	orange juice
½ tsp.	½ tsp.	½ tsp.	salt
175g	6 oz	1 cup	fresh or frozen blueberries

Preheat the oven to 180°C/350°F/Gas mark 4
Use a 900g/2 lb loaf tin.

Grease and line the loaf tin. Beat the butter, sugar and sour cream together until light and fluffy. Stir in the orange rind.

Mix the milk and orange juice. Sift the dry ingredients together and add to the first mixture alternately with milk-orange juice mixture. Blend well after each addition. Fold in the blueberries. Put the mixture into the loaf tin and bake for 50 to 60 minutes. Allow to cool for ten minutes in the tin before turning out onto a wire rack to cool completely.

Pineapple Nut Bread

METRIC	IMP.	US.	
275g	10 oz	2 ½ cups	white self-raising flour
75g	3 oz	¾ cup	nuts, chopped
1 ½ tsp.	1 ½ tsp.	1 ½ tsp.	baking powder
125ml	8 tbs.	½ cup	milk
175g	6 oz	¾ cup	brown sugar
½ tsp.	½ tsp.	½ tsp.	salt
175g	6 oz	1 ½ cups	All Bran
175g	6 oz	1 cup	undrained pineapple pieces
6 tbs.	6 tbs.	6 tbs.	melted butter

Preheat the oven to 180°C/350°F/Gas mark 4
Use a 900g/2 lb loaf tin.

Grease and line the loaf tin. Combine the dry ingredients in a bowl. Add the nuts, All Bran, pineapple, and butter. Mix thoroughly. Add milk. Put into the loaf tin and bake for 60 minutes. Leave to cool in the tin for 10 minutes before turning out to cool completely on a wire rack.

Pear and Nut Cake

METRIC	IMP.	US.	
100g	4 oz	1 cup	wholemeal self-raising flour
100g	4 oz	1 cup	white self-raising white flour
575g	1 ¼ lb	1 ¾ lb	ripe pears, peeled and cored
1 tsp.	1 tsp.	1 tsp.	baking powder
6 tbs.	6 tbs.	6 tbs.	butter
3 tbs.	3 tbs.	3 tbs.	golden syrup
4 tbs.	4 tbs.	4 tbs.	sour cream
1 tsp.	1 tsp.	1 tsp.	ground mace
50g	2 oz	½ cup	shelled walnuts, chopped

Preheat the oven to 190°C/375°F/Gas mark 5
Use an 18cm/7 inch round cake tin.

Line and grease the cake tin. Puree three-quarters of the pears in a blender or food processor until smooth. Thinly slice the remaining pears and reserve.

Cream the butter and syrup together, then gradually add the sour cream, flours, baking powder, mace and walnuts. Mix in the pear puree. Put half the mixture in the prepared tin, lay the reserved pear slices on top and cover with the remaining mixture. Bake in for about 1 hour or until a warm knife inserted into the centre comes out clean. Cool in the tin for ten minutes before turning out.

Fig and Apple Loaf

METRIC	IMP.	US.	
225g	8 oz	2 cups	white self-raising flour
100g	4 oz	¾ cup	cooking apples, chopped
100g	4 oz	¾ cup	dried figs, chopped
100g	4 oz	½ cup	butter
100g	4 oz	½ cup	dark brown soft sugar
4 tbs.	4 tbs.	4 tbs.	sour cream
			rind and juice of 1 lemon

Preheat the oven to 160°C/325°F/Gas mark 3
Use a 900g/2 lb loaf tin.

Peel, core and chop the apples and place with the figs and 3 tbs. of water in the saucepan with rind and juice. Cook over a gentle heat until the mixture becomes a soft puree. Beat well and leave to cool.

Grease and line the loaf tin. Cream together the butter and sugar until light and fluffy. Gradually beat in the sour cream, then lightly beat in the flour. Spoon one-third of the cake mixture into the prepared tin and spread it evenly over the base. Spread half of the fig mixture on top. Repeat the layering, finishing with cake mixture on top. Bake for about 1 hour 10 minutes or until well risen and firm to the touch. Cover with foil half-way through cooking if the loaf browns too quickly. Turn out and cool on a wire rack.

Tuscan Persimmon Cake

Persimmons used in this Italian delicacy must be soft and ripe. Quarter the fruit and scoop out the flesh with a spoon.

METRIC	IMP.	US	
10	10	10	ripe persimmons, mashed
75g	3 oz	½ cup	almonds, chopped
75g	3 oz	½ cup	walnuts, chopped
40g	1 ½ oz	¼ cup	peanuts, chopped
12 tbs.	12 tbs.	12 tbs.	pine-nuts
125g	4 oz	½ cup	brown sugar
350g	12 oz	3 cups	plain flour
50g	2 oz	¼ cup	butter
1 tsp.	1 tsp.	1 tsp.	baking powder
1 tsp.	1 tsp.	1 tsp.	grated lemon rind

Preheat the oven to 180°C/350°F/Gas mark 4
Use a 20cm/8 inch cake tin.

Grease the cake tin and coat with flour. Stir the walnuts, almonds, peanuts and pine-nuts into the persimmon flesh in a large bowl. Cream together the sugar and butter. Stir into the persimmon mixture. Sift in the flour and baking powder. Add the grated lemon rind. Stir until well blended. Bake in the preheated oven for 40 minutes, or until a warm knife inserted in the centre comes out clean. Leave in the tin to cool for 15 minutes, before turning out onto a wire rack to cool completely.

Pineapple Tea Bread

METRIC	IMP.	US.	
350g	12 oz	3 cups	white self-raising flour
1 tsp.	1 tsp.	1 tsp.	baking powder
175g	6 oz	¾ cup	butter
175g	6 oz	¾ cup	soft brown sugar
75g	3 oz	½ cup	sultanas
175g	6 oz	1 cup	fresh pineapple, chopped
4 tbs.	4 tbs.	4 tbs.	sour cream
125ml	8 tbs.	½ cup	milk
½ tsp.	½ tsp.	½ tsp.	pineapple essence (optional)
12	12	12	sugar cubes, to decorate

Preheat the oven to 180°C/350°F/Gas mark 4
Use a 900g/2 lb loaf tin.

Grease and line the loaf tin. Rub the butter into the flour, add the sugar, sultanas and pineapple. Mix the sour cream, milk and essence (if using) together. Pour on to the dry ingredients and mix to a soft dropping consistency.

Turn into the prepared tin and level the surface. Roughly crush the sugar cubes and scatter over the top. Bake for about 1 ¼ hours or until well risen and firm to the touch. Turn out and cool on a wire rack.

Apple and Walnut Teabread

METRIC	IMP.	US.	
225g	8 oz	2 cups	white self-raising flour
½ tsp.	½ tsp.	½ tsp.	baking powder
100g	4 oz	½ cup	butter
100g	4 oz	½ cup	brown sugar
4 tbs.	4 tbs.	4 tbs.	sour cream
1 tbs.	1 tbs.	1 tbs.	golden syrup
75g	3 oz	½ cup	sultanas
50g	2 oz	½ cup	walnuts, chopped
1 tsp.	1 tsp.	1 tsp.	ground mixed spice
1	1	1	medium cooking apple
			icing sugar, for dredging

Preheat the oven to 180°C/350°F/Gas mark 4
Use a 900g/2 lb loaf tin.

Peel, core and chop the apple. Grease the loaf tin and line with greaseproof paper. Place all the ingredients except the icing sugar in a large bowl and beat with a wooden spoon until well combined. Turn into the prepared tin and level the surface. Bake for 1 hour. Reduce the oven temperature to 170C/325F/gas mark 3 for a further 20 minutes or until well risen and firm to the touch. Turn out and cool on a wire rack. When cold, dredge with icing sugar.

Vegan Apple Cake

METRIC	IMP.	US.	
225g	8 oz	2 cups	wholemeal self-raising flour
1 tsp.	1 tsp.	1 tsp.	baking powder
100g	4 oz	½ cup	soft vegetable margarine
6 tbs.	6 tbs.	6 tbs.	dark brown sugar
2	2	2	dessert apples, grated
1 tbs.	1 tbs.	1 tbs.	soya flour
1 tbs.	1 tbs.	1 tbs.	wheat germ
1 tbs.	1 tbs.	1 tbs.	ground cinnamon
75g	3 oz	½ cup	sultanas
2 tbs.	2 tbs.	2 tbs.	soya milk
			juice of 1 lemon
			water if necessary

Preheat the oven to 190°C/375°F/Gas mark 5
Use a 20cm/8 inch sandwich tin.

Oil and line the cake tin. Cream the margarine and sugar together for 5 minutes or until light and fluffy. Stir in the apples. Mix together the flours, wheat germ, cinnamon, baking powder and sultanas. Stir this into the creamed margarine and apples and add the soya milk and lemon juice. Add a little water if the batter is too thick. Pour the batter into the sandwich tin. Bake for 40 minutes to 1 hour in the preheated oven. The cake is baked when a warm knife inserted into it comes out clean. Remove the cake from the tin and allow to cool on a wire rack.

Apricot Upside-Down Cake

FOR THE CAKE

METRIC	IMP.	US.	
50g	2 oz	½ cup	cornflour
175g	6 oz	1 ½ cups	white self-raising flour
½ tsp.	½ tsp.	½ tsp.	baking powder
¾ kg	1 ½ lb	4 cups	fresh apricots
100g	4 oz	½ cup	caster sugar
4 tbs.	4 tbs.	4 tbs.	sour cream
100g	4 oz	½ cup	butter
1 tbs.	1 tbs.	1 tbs.	ground almonds

SYRUP

METRIC	IMP.	US.	
275g	10 oz	1 ¼ cups	sugar
600ml	1 pint	2 ½ cups	water

CARAMEL

METRIC	IMP.	US.	
175g	6 oz	¾ cup	sugar
125ml.	4 fl. oz.	½ cup	water

Preheat the oven to 190°C/375°F/Gas mark 5
Use a 23cm/9 inch square cake tin.

Syrup: Make a syrup by boiling the sugar with 600ml/1 pint of water for 5 minutes.

Caramel: Put the sugar into a pan with 10 tbs. or ½ cup of water. Stir over low heat until dissolved, then boil hard to a rich caramel brown (don't stir, but watch it). Wrap your hand in a tea towel, and stir in - off the heat - 4 tbs. water, using a wooden spoon. The caramel will sizzle, harden and look very odd. Just stir carefully, and if it does not dissolve into a clear smooth caramel, put it back over the heat until it does. Pour into the lightly greased cake tin and set aside.

Bring the syrup to the boil in a wide pan, and slip in the halved stoned apricots, cut side down. When the syrup returns to the boil, give it a minute to simmer, then turn the apricots over. By this time, they will be cooked enough. Do not let them collapse. Remove with a slotted spoon and pack closely together, cut side down, on top of the caramel.

Lightly grease the cake tin. Put all the cake ingredients into the bowl of an electric mixer or processor and whizz until smoothly blended. If necessary, add a couple of tbs. of the apricot syrup to make the mixture a dropping consistency. The ingredients can equally well be beaten together by hand; make sure the butter is very soft indeed.

Spread carefully and evenly over the apricots. Bake for about 45 minutes. The top should brown nicely. Cool for a moment, then run a warm knife round the edge, put a serving plate on top and quickly turn upside down. Serve warm, with fresh cream.

If you like, you can split and toast as many almonds as there are apricots, and put a nice brown piece in the cavity of each half of apricot.

Passion Fruit Tea Bread

METRIC	IMP.	US.	
175g	6 oz	1 ½ cups	white self-raising flour
pinch.	pinch.	pinch.	salt
100g	4 oz	½ cup	caster sugar
100g	4 oz	½ cup	butter
6 tbs.	6 tbs.	6 tbs.	sour cream
50g	2 oz	¼ cup	passion fruit pulp
6 tbs.	6 tbs.	6 tbs.	cold milk
1 tbs.	1 tbs.	1 tbs.	finely grated
			lemon rind
			icing sugar for dusting

Preheat the oven to 180°C/350°F/Gas mark 4
Use a 900g/2 lb loaf tin.

Grease and flour the baking tin. Sift the flour and salt. Cream the sugar and butter until light in colour and fluffy. Whisk the sour cream, passion-fruit pulp and milk together and beat into the creamy mixture.

Fold in the lemon rind and flour. Spoon the mixture into the prepared tin, level the top and bake for 55-60 minutes, or until a warm knife inserted into the centre comes out clean. Cool in the tin for 10 minutes before turning out to cool on a wire rack. Dust with icing sugar and allow to become completely cold before slicing.

Pear and Cinnamon Loaf

METRIC	IMP.	US.	
225g	8 oz	2 cups	white self-raising flour
100g	4 oz	½ cup	light soft brown sugar
4 tbs.	4 tbs.	4 tbs.	butter
2 tbs.	2 tbs.	2 tbs.	sour cream
125ml	8 tbs.	½ cup	milk
2 tsp.	2 tsp.	2 tsp.	ground cinnamon
1	1	1	large firm pear, finely chopped
50g	2 oz	½ cup	chopped walnuts

Preheat the oven to 180°C/350°F/Gas mark 4
Use a 900g/2 lb loaf tin.

Grease and line the base and sides of the loaf tin. In a small pan, melt the sugar and butter over a low heat. Set aside to cool. Pour the melted butter and sugar into a large mixing bowl and stir in the sour cream and milk. Sift the flour and cinnamon into the mixture, and stir in, then beat well. Lastly, add the chopped pears and walnuts.

Pour the mixture into the tin and bake for about 1 ½ hours, or until the loaf starts to shrink from the sides of the tin. Allow to cool and firm up in the tin, then remove, using the lining paper to lift it out, peel off paper and cool on a wire tray.

GIFTS FOR DIWALI.

LIGHT DRIED FRUIT CAKES.

Diwali, the New Year celebration for Hindus is in November. Devotees welcome the return of Rama to His kingdom of Ayodhya, after rescuing His wife Sita, from the clutches of the evil Ravana.

Diwali is a time of giving and sharing, and *Vaishnavas* at Bhaktivedanta Manor take advantage of the occasion to offer prasadam, food sanctified by the Lord, to supporters and friends who have helped the temple throughout the year.

This is no small time operation, but is carried out with military precision. In the forefront of the effort, is Ananda Vigraha, a Gujerati devotee who has made baking her life and soul. During the run-up to Diwali, Ananda will single-handedly bake close to 3000 small cakes which are boxed and taken to supporters by the students and priests.

Ananda is the chief baker for all occasions. My first sample of her art was at a wedding at the Manor. She had made a light fruit cake with a moist balanced composition and a full flavour. This was an eye-opener for me. My previous experience of devotee baking was the infamous Black Velvet cake, ostensibly Carob flavoured, but with more than a hint of bicarb.

Ananda's talents go beyond the oven. It's noticeable that on the days she makes lunch for the community, there are a lot of extra diners. She is never conceited and is always willing to instruct, to share and to learn. Her latest venture is to pass on the art of devotional cooking to the eager members at the new Budapest Hare Krishna centre.

Taking to spiritual life does not mean that troubles fly away and leave us skipping along the golden road to heaven. There are always personal challenges to be won. Knowing that there are humble Vaishnavis like Ananda, gives me a boost when dark clouds appear on the horizon.

Akinchana.

Date and Walnut Cake (Vegan)

METRIC	IMP.	US.	
225g	8 oz	2 cups	white self-raising flour
100g	4 oz	¾ cup	dates, chopped
1 tsp.	1 tsp.	1 tsp.	bicarb.
100g	4 oz	½ cup	light muscovado sugar
4 tbs.	4 tbs.	4 tbs.	soft vegetable margarine
2 tbs.	2 tbs.	2 tbs.	soya milk
250ml	8 fl. oz	1 cup	boiling water
50g	2 oz	½ cup	walnuts, chopped

Preheat the oven to 180°C/350°F/Gas mark 4
Use a 20cm/8 inch square cake tin.

Grease and line the cake tin with greased greaseproof paper. Measure the water, dates and bicarb. into a bowl and leave to stand for about 5 minutes. Put the sugar and margarine into a bowl and cream together, then beat in the soya milk and the date mixture. Fold in the flour together with the walnuts and mix lightly until thoroughly blended. Turn the mixture into the tin and level out evenly.

Bake in the oven for about an hour until risen and slightly shrinking away from the sides of the tin. A warm knife should come out clean when inserted into the centre of the cake. Leave to cool in the tin for five minutes, then turn out. Peel off paper and finish cooling on a wire rack.

Sultana Special

METRIC	IMP.	US.	
225g	8 oz	2 cups	white self-raising flour
1 tsp.	1 tsp.	1 tsp.	baking powder
1 tsp.	1 tsp.	1 tsp.	ground cinnamon
100g	4 oz	½ cup	butter
4 tbs.	4 tbs.	4 tbs.	caster sugar
75g	3 oz	½ cup	currants
75g	3 oz	½ cup	sultanas
125ml	8 tbs.	½ cup	fresh milk
3 tbs.	3 tbs.	3 tbs.	golden syrup

Preheat the oven to 160°C/325°F/Gas mark 3
Use a 15cm/6 inch round cake tin.

Grease and line the cake tin. Put the butter, flour, baking powder and cinnamon in a bowl and rub together until the mixture resembles fine breadcrumbs. Add fruit and sugar and stir thoroughly. Make a well in the centre of the mixture. Mix the golden syrup and the milk and pour this into the centre. Gradually mix together, adding a bit more milk if necessary to attain a dropping consistency. Pour the mixture into the prepared cake tin and bake in the preset oven for 1 ¾ to 2 hours or until the cake is well risen and firm to touch. Remove from the oven and allow to stand for ten minutes. Turn out onto cooling rack.

Walnut and Fruit Cake

METRIC	IMP.	US.	
225g	8 oz	2 cups	white self-raising flour
1 tsp.	1 tsp.	1 tsp.	bicarb.
6 tbs.	6 tbs.	6 tbs.	butter
175g	6 oz	¾ cup	mixed fruit
175g	6 oz	¾ cup	soft brown sugar
250ml	8 fl. oz	1 cup	water
50g	2 oz	½ cup	walnuts chopped
½ tsp.	½ tsp.	½ tsp.	salt
½ tsp.	½ tsp.	½ tsp.	cinnamon
½ tsp.	½ tsp.	½ tsp.	mixed spice
¼ tsp.	¼ tsp.	¼ tsp.	nutmeg
4 tbs.	4 tbs.	4 tbs.	sour cream

Preheat the oven to 180°C/350°F/Gas mark 4
Use an 18cm/7 inch loose bottom cake tin.

Grease and line the cake tin. Place the fruit and water in a saucepan and bring to a boil. Cover, reduce heat and simmer for 10 minutes. Add the sugar and butter and stir until the butter melts. Remove from the heat and cool.

Sift the flour, spices and soda in a large mixing bowl. Add the walnuts and mix. Make a well in the centre of the dry ingredients. Add the wet ingredients and the sour cream, beating until well mixed. Spoon the mixture into the prepared tin and bake for 1 hour and 20 minutes, until well risen. Leave in tin for 10 minutes, then turn out onto wire rack to cool.

Everyday Fruit Cake

METRIC	IMP.	US.	
225g	8 oz	2 cups	white self-raising flour
½ tsp.	½ tsp.	½ tsp.	baking powder
100g	4 oz	½ cup	soft brown sugar
100g	4 oz	½ cup	butter
½ tsp.	½ tsp.	½ tsp.	ground mixed spice
½ tsp.	½ tsp.	½ tsp.	ground cinnamon
75g	3 oz	½ cup	sultanas
75g	3 oz	½ cup	currants
50g	2 oz	¼ cup	glacé cherries, quartered
2 tbs.	2 tbs.	2 tbs.	sour cream
125ml	8 tbs.	½ cup	milk

Preheat the oven to 180°C/350°F/Gas mark 4
Use a deep 15cm/6 inch cake tin.

Grease and line the cake tin. Sift the flour and spices into a mixing bowl, and rub in the butter until the mixture resembles fine breadcrumbs. Stir in the fruit and sugar. Mix the sour cream and milk together, and add to the mixture. Beat thoroughly. Place in the prepared tin and bake for 1 ¼ to 1 ½ hrs. Leave in the tin for ten minutes, then turn onto wire rack to cool completely.

Old English Cherry Cake

METRIC	IMP.	US.	
225g	8 oz	2 cups	white self-raising flour
½ tsp.	½ tsp.	½ tsp.	baking powder
100g	4 oz	½ cup	soft butter
100g	4 oz	½ cup	caster sugar
2 tbs.	2 tbs.	2 tbs.	sour cream
100g	4 oz	½ cup	glacé cherries, quartered
125ml.	4 fl. oz.	½ cup	milk

Preheat the oven to 160°C/325°F/Gas mark 3
Use an 18cm/7 inch deep round cake tin.

Be sure to wash the cherries and then dry them thoroughly before adding to the mixture. This stops them from sinking to the bottom of the cake during baking.

Grease and line the cake tin. Measure all the ingredients into a bowl and beat well until thoroughly blended. Turn the mixture into the prepared tin and level out evenly.

Bake in the oven for about 1 ½ hours or until a warm knife inserted into the centre of the cake comes out clean. Leave to cool in the tin for 5 minutes, then turn out, peel off paper and finish cooling on a wire rack.

Coningdale Cake

METRIC	*IMP.*	*US.*	
425g	15 oz	3 ¾ cups	white self-raising flour
2 tsp.	2 tsp.	2 tsp.	baking powder
1 tsp.	1 tsp.	1 tsp.	mixed spice
225g	8 oz	1 cup	butter
4 tbs.	4 tbs.	4 tbs.	firmly packed brown sugar
175g	6 oz	1 cup	raisins
175g	6 oz	1 cup	sultanas
2 tbs.	2 tbs.	2 tbs.	chopped mixed peel
2 tbs.	2 tbs.	2 tbs.	sour cream
300ml	½ pint	1 ¼ cups	milk to mix

Preheat the oven to 180°C/350°F/Gas mark 4
Use a 20cm/8 inch deep cake tin.

Grease and line the cake tin. Sift the flour with the baking powder and spice into a bowl and rub in the butter until crumbly. Add brown sugar, raisins, sultanas and mixed peel and mix well. Stir in sour cream and enough milk to make a soft dropping mixture, pour into the cake tin and bake for 1 ¾ - 2 hours or until golden brown. Test with a warm knife. Turn on to a wire rack, right side up, to cool, then store in an airtight container.

Apricot Cake.

METRIC	IMP.	US.	
400g	14 oz	3 ½ cups	white self-raising flour
225g	8 oz	1 cups	caster sugar
360ml	12 fl. oz	1 ½ cups	milk
4 tbs.	4 tbs.	4 tbs.	sour cream
1 tsp.	1 tsp.	1 tsp.	ground cloves
1 tbs.	1 tbs.	1 tbs.	ground cinnamon
2 tbs.	2 tbs.	2 tbs.	carob powder
175g	6 oz	½ cup	apricot jam
100g	4 oz	1 cup	nuts, chopped
75g	3 oz	½ cup	seedless raisins
6	6	6	dried apricots, chopped

Preheat the oven to 180°C/350°F/Gas mark 4
Use a 25cm/10 inch cake tin.

Grease and line the tin. Put 175g/6 oz of sugar in a saucepan and heat over a low flame until it caramelises. Add the milk and stir. When the caramel is melted add the rest of the sugar and cool. Add the sour cream, flour, cloves, cinnamon, carob and the jam and mix well. Finally, add the nuts, raisins and apricots. Pour the batter into the cake tin and bake in a preheated oven for about 40-50 minutes.

Fat-Free Fig Loaf (Vegan)

METRIC	IMP.	US.	
225g	8 oz	2 cups	wholemeal self-raising flour
250g	9 oz	1 ½ cups	dried figs, chopped
100g	4 oz	½ cup	soft brown sugar
225g	8 oz	2 cups	All Bran
2 tbs.	2 tbs.	2 tbs.	black treacle
600ml	1 pint	2 cups	apple juice
2 tsp.	2 tsp.	2 tsp.	baking powder

Preheat the oven to 180°C/350°F/Gas mark 4
Use a 900g/2 lb loaf tin.

Greasc and line the loaf tin. Place the All-bran, treacle and apple juice in a mixing bowl and leave to stand for 1 hour. Sift in the baking powder, add the remaining ingredients and mix well.

Turn into the loaf tin and bake for 1 ¼ to 1 ½ hours. Turn on a wire rack to cool.

Date Loaf (Vegan)

METRIC	IMP.	US.	
225g	8 oz	2 cups	wholemeal self-raising flour
1 tsp.	1 tsp.	1 tsp.	baking powder
250g	9 oz	1 ½ cups	chopped dates
125ml	8 tbs.	½ cup	apple juice
2 tsp.	2 tsp.	2 tsp.	baking powder
1 tsp.	1 tsp.	1 tsp.	ground mixed spice
100g	4 oz	½ cup	soft brown sugar
125ml	8 tbs.	½ cup	soya milk
1 tsp.	1 tsp.	1 tsp.	demerara sugar for sprinkling

Preheat the oven to 180°C/350°F/Gas mark 4
Use a 900g/2 lb loaf tin.

Grease and line the loaf tin. Put the dates in a bowl, pour the apple juice over and leave to soak for 2 hours. Sift in the baking powder, add the remaining ingredients and mix thoroughly.

Turn into the loaf tin. Sprinkle with the demerara sugar and bake for 1 to 1 ¼ hours.

Fruit and Nut Cake

METRIC	IMP.	US.	
225g	8 oz	2 cups	white self-raising flour
½ tsp.	½ tsp.	½ tsp.	baking powder
75g	3 oz	½ cup	chopped raisins
75g	3 oz	½ cup	currants, washed and dried
75g	3 oz	½ cup	walnut pieces, chopped
175g	6 oz	¾ cup	butter, cut into small pieces
1 tbs.	1 tbs.	1 tbs.	black treacle, warmed
125ml	8 tbs.	½ cup	milk
6 tbs.	6 tbs.	6 tbs.	brown sugar
2 tbs.	2 tbs.	2 tbs.	lemon juice

Preheat the oven to 160°C/325°F/Gas mark 3
Use a 15cm/6 inch square tin.

Lightly grease the cake tin. Put the raisins, currants and walnuts into a small mixing bowl and mix thoroughly. Sift the flour and baking powder into another bowl and rub in the butter until the mixture resembles coarse breadcrumbs. Add the fruit and nuts, treacle, milk and sugar. Using a spatula, fold so that there are no dry pockets of flour. Lastly, very lightly fold in the lemon juice.

Pour this mixture into the tin and level it off. Bake for about 1 ¼ to 1 ½ hours, or until the cake is shrinking from the sides of the tin. Allow to firm up in the tin for 10 minutes, then turn out, peel off the lining paper and cool on a wire tray.

East Coast Prune Bread

Prune bread is a traditional American fruit loaf from the East Coast. The following recipe can be varied by substituting dried apricots, persimmons or pears for prunes.

METRIC	IMP.	US.	
200g	7 oz	1 ¾ cups	white self-raising flour
75g	3 oz	¾ cup	wholemeal self-raising flour
2 tsp.	2 tsp.	2 tsp.	cinnamon
2 tsp.	2 tsp.	2 tsp.	baking powder
6 tbs.	6 tbs.	6 tbs.	butter
75g	3 oz	¼ cup	golden syrup
¼ tsp.	¼ tsp.	¼ tsp.	vanilla essence
175g	6 oz	¾ cup	chopped, cooked prunes
250ml	8 fl. oz	1 cup	sour cream
			grated rind of one lemon

Preheat the oven to 180°C/350°F/Gas mark 4
Use a 900g/2 lb loaf tin.

Grease the loaf tin. Sift the dry ingredients together into a bowl and stir in the wholemeal flour. Cream the butter and golden syrup and then whisk in the vanilla and lemon rind. Toss the chopped prunes in the bowl of flour and coat well. Fold in the golden syrup mixture alternately with the sour cream. Fill the loaf tin with the batter. Bake for about 1 hour or until a warm knife, inserted into the centre of the prune bread comes away clean.

Apricot Bran Bread

METRIC	IMP.	US.	
175g	6 oz	1 ½ cups	white self-raising flour
1 tsp.	1 tsp.	1 tsp.	baking powder
175g	6 oz	¾ cup	brown sugar
3 tbs.	3 tbs.	3 tbs.	sugar
1 tsp.	1 tsp.	1 tsp.	salt
150g	5 oz	1 cup	whole bran cereal
250g	9 oz	1 ½ cups	chopped dried apricots
300ml	½ pint	1 ¼ cups	milk
4 tbs.	4 tbs.	4 tbs.	sour cream
125ml	8 tbs.	½ cup	cooking oil
			a little sugar for sprinkling
			boiling water

Preheat the oven to 180°C/350°F/Gas mark 4
Use a 900g/2 lb loaf tin.

Grease the loaf tin. Pour enough boiling water over the chopped apricots to cover. Allow to stand for 10 minutes. Drain well. Combine the apricots and the 3 tbs. of sugar. Sift together the flour, the brown sugar, the baking powder and salt. Mix the bran cereal, milk, sour cream, and oil. Add to the sifted ingredients, stirring till just moistened. Gently stir in apricot mixture. Turn into the loaf tin. Sprinkle top with a little additional sugar. Bake for about 1 hour. Test with a warm knife. leave to firm up in the tin for ten minutes, before turning out.

Golden Fruit Cake

METRIC	IMP.	US.	
225g	8 oz	2 cups	white self-raising flour
100g	4 oz	½ cup	light brown sugar
½ tsp.	½ tsp.	½ tsp.	baking powder
½ tsp.	½ tsp.	½ tsp.	ground cinnamon
¼ tsp.	¼ tsp.	¼ tsp.	grated nutmeg
¼ tsp.	¼ tsp.	¼ tsp.	ground ginger
1 tbs.	1 tbs.	1 tbs.	full-cream milk powder
225g	8 oz	1 ½ cups	cooked and mashed pumpkin
2 tbs.	2 tbs.	2 tbs.	golden syrup
4 tbs.	4 tbs.	4 tbs.	sour cream
125ml	8 tbs.	½ cup	corn oil
250g	9 oz	1 ½ cups	chopped raisins
3 tbs.	3 tbs.	3 tbs.	water

Preheat the oven to 180°C/350°F/Gas mark 4
Use an oblong cake tin 23 x 13 cm/9 x 5 inches.

Line and grease the cake tin. Beat the sugar, sour cream and oil in a large bowl for 2 minutes. Add the pumpkin and golden syrup and beat again until well mixed. Sift the flour, spices and milk powder together, then sift again into the sugar-pumpkin mixture. Using a wooden spoon, fold through lightly. Add the raisins and water and fold again. Turn into the cake tin.

Bake for 1 hour, then reduce the temperature slightly and bake for a further 20 to 30 minutes. Remove from the oven and allow to stand for 10 minutes before turning out onto a cake rack to cool. Best if left to stand overnight.

Buttermilk Fruit Loaf

METRIC	IMP.	US.	
175g	6 oz	1 ½ cups	white self-raising flour
1 tsp.	1 tsp.	1 tsp.	baking powder
6 tbs.	6 tbs.	6 tbs.	brown sugar
75g	3 oz	¼ cup	golden syrup
4 tbs.	4 tbs.	4 tbs.	butter, softened
2 tbs.	2 tbs.	2 tbs.	sour cream
¼ tsp.	¼ tsp.	¼ tsp.	salt
75g	3 oz	½ cup	sultanas
250ml	8 fl. oz	1 cup	buttermilk
75g	3 oz	¾ cup	porridge oats

Preheat the oven to 160°C/325°F/Gas mark 3
Use a 900g/2 lb loaf tin.

Line and grease the tin. Beat the sugar, syrup and butter in a bowl until soft and creamy. Add the sour cream and mix. Sift the flour, baking powder and salt into the butter mixture and fold in. Add the sultanas and stir through. Mix the milk and oats together. Fold into the mixture in the bowl. Mix thoroughly to combine. Spoon into the loaf tin. Bake for 55 to 60 minutes. Remove from the oven and allow to stand for 10 minutes before turning out onto a cake rack to cool.

Yoghurt Fig Loaf

METRIC	IMP.	US.	
225g	8 oz	2 cups	white self-raising flour
1 tsp.	1 tsp.	1 tsp.	baking powder
100g	4 oz	½ cup	dark brown soft sugar
125ml	8 tbs.	½ cup	orange juice
250g	9 oz	1 ½ cups	dried figs, chopped
2 tbs.	2 tbs.	2 tbs.	sour cream
125ml	8 tbs.	½ cup	natural yoghurt

Preheat the oven to 180°C/350°F/Gas mark 4
Use a 900g/2 lb loaf tin.

Grease and line the tin. Put the orange juice, figs and sugar in a bowl and soak for 1 hour. Mix the remaining ingredients into the soaked figs and beat together thoroughly. Spoon the mixture into the prepared tin and bake in the oven for 1 ¼ - 1 ½ hours or until a warm knife inserted in the centre comes out clean. Leave to cool in the tin for 10 mins. then turn out on a wire rack.

Rosewater Currant Ring

METRIC	IMP.	US.	
225g	8 oz	2 cups	wholemeal self-raising flour
1 tsp.	1 tsp.	1 tsp.	baking powder
½ tsp.	½ tsp.	½ tsp.	ground cinnamon
100g	4 oz	1 cup	desiccated coconut
175g	6 oz	¾ cup	brown sugar
4 tbs.	4 tbs.	4 tbs.	sour cream
125ml	8 tbs.	½ cup	vegetable oil
3 tbs.	3 tbs.	3 tbs.	rosewater
250g	9 oz	1 ½ cups	currants

Preheat the oven to 180°C/350°F/Gas mark 4
Grease a deep 8 inch ring tin.

Grease the ring tin. Soak the currants in boiling water for 20 minutes. Beat together the sugar and sour cream then beat in the oil and rosewater. Drain the currants (reserve the water) and add the currants to the mixture. Stir in the coconut. Sift the flour, baking powder and cinnamon together, then fold this into the sugar-cream-mixture, with 90-125ml/3-4 fl oz of the currant-soaking water. Pour into the tin and level the top. Bake for 45 minutes. Allow to cool before turning out of the tin. For extra flavour the cake can be spread with thin simple icing.

Tyrol Cake

METRIC	IMP.	US.	
225g	8 oz	2 cups	white self-raising flour
½ tsp.	½ tsp.	½ tsp.	baking powder
100g	4 oz	½ cup	butter
1 tsp.	1 tsp.	1 tsp.	ground cinnamon
4 tbs.	4 tbs.	4 tbs.	caster sugar
75g	3 oz	½ cup	currants
75g	3 oz	½ cup	sultanas
125ml	8 tbs.	½ cup	milk
3 tbs.	3 tbs.	3 tbs.	golden syrup

Preheat the oven to 160°C/325°F/Gas mark 3
Use a 15cm/6 inch round cake tin.

Grease and line the tin. Mix the butter, flour, baking powder and cinnamon in a bowl until the mixture resembles fine bread crumbs. Add the washed fruit and sugar to the mixture and stir thoroughly. Make a well in the centre. Mix the milk and syrup and pour this into the well. Gradually work in all the dry ingredients, adding a little more milk if needed, just sufficient to give the mixture a dropping consistency. Pour the mixture into the prepared tin and bake for 1 ¾ to 2 hours or until the cake is well risen and firm to the touch.

Malted Fruit Loaf

METRIC	IMP.	US.	
350g	12 oz	3 cups	white self-raising flour
2 tsp.	2 tsp.	2 tsp.	baking powder
250g	9 oz	1 ½ cups	sultanas
2 tbs.	2 tbs.	2 tbs.	demerara sugar
9 tbs.	9 tbs.	9 tbs.	malt extract
4 tbs.	4 tbs.	4 tbs.	sour cream
300ml	½ pint	1 ¼ cups	fresh apple juice

Preheat the oven to 150°C/300°F/Gas mark 2
Use a 900g/2 lb loaf tin.

This loaf is cooked covered with a weighted lid to give the traditional malt bread texture and shape. Grease and line the loaf tin. Grease the underside of a baking sheet. Sift the flour and baking powder together in a bowl. Stir in the sultanas. Slowly heat together the demerara sugar and malt extract. Do not boil. Pour on to the dry ingredients. Add the sour cream and apple juice and beat well. Turn the mixture into the prepared tin. Cover with the baking sheet, greased side down. Place a weight on top. Bake in the oven for about 1 ½ hours. Turn out and cool on a wire rack. Taste improves with keeping.

Rosehip Teabread (Vegan)

METRIC	IMP.	US.	
75g	3 oz	¾ cup	white self-raising flour
75g	3 oz	¾ cup	self-raising wholemeal flour
½ tsp.	½ tsp.	½ tsp.	baking powder
75g	3 oz	½ cup	seedless raisins
75g	3 oz	½ cup	sultanas
75g	3 oz	½ cup	mixed peel
2 tbs.	2 tbs.	2 tbs.	soya milk
4 tbs.	4 tbs.	4 tbs.	light brown soft sugar
300ml	½ pint	1 ¼ cups	strained cold rosehip tea

Preheat the oven to 180°C/350°F/Gas mark 4
Use a 450g/1 lb loaf tin.

Soak the tea, raisins, sultanas and mixed peel overnight.

Lightly grease the loaf tin and line with greaseproof paper. Add the soya milk, flours, sugar and baking powder to the tea and plumped fruit. Mix well and pour into the prepared tin. Bake in the oven for 1 hour or until the cake shrinks away from the sides of the tin and feels firm to the touch. Leave for ten minutes to firm up in the tin, before turning out on to a wire rack to cool completely.

For a variation, try other herbal teas, Peppermint for example.

Farmhouse Sultana Cake

METRIC	IMP.	US.	
100g	4 oz	1 cup	white self-raising flour
100g	4 oz	1 cup	wholemeal self-raising flour
2 tsp.	2 tsp.	2 tsp.	mixed spice
2 tsp.	2 tsp.	2 tsp.	baking powder
1 tsp.	1 tsp.	1 tsp.	bicarb.
175g	6 oz	¾ cup	butter
225g	8 oz	1 cup	dark brown soft sugar
250g	9 oz	1 ½ cups	sultanas
4 tbs.	4 tbs.	4 tbs.	sour cream
10	10	10	sugar cubes, to decorate
250ml	8 fl. oz	1 cup	milk (approx).

Preheat the oven to 160°C/325°F/Gas mark 3
Use a deep 20cm/8 inch loose bottom cake tin.

Grease and line the cake tin. Sift the white flour, spice, baking powder and bicarb. into a large bowl and stir in the wholemeal flour. Rub in the butter until the mixture resembles fine breadcrumbs and stir in the sugar and sultanas.

Make a well in the centre and gradually pour in the sour cream and milk. Beat gently until well mixed and of a soft dropping consistency, adding more milk if necessary. Turn the mixture into the prepared tin and level the surface. Roughly crush the sugar cubes and scatter over the cake. Bake in the oven for about 1 hour 40 minutes or until a warm knife inserted into the centre comes out clean. Turn out to cool on a wire rack.

Prune and Nut Loaf

METRIC	IMP.	US.	
275g	10 oz	2 ½ cups	white self-raising flour
1 tsp.	1 tsp.	1 tsp.	baking powder
½ tsp.	½ tsp.	½ tsp.	bicarb.
pinch.	pinch.	pinch.	of salt
2 tsp.	2 tsp.	2 tsp.	ground cinnamon
100g	4 oz	½ cup	butter
100g	4 oz	1 cup	demerara sugar
2 tbs.	2 tbs.	2 tbs.	sour cream
125ml	8 tbs.	½ cup	milk
50g	2 oz	½ cup	walnuts, chopped
100g	4 oz	½ cup	no-soak prunes, chopped
1 tbs.	1 tbs.	1 tbs.	honey

Preheat the oven to 190°C/375°F/Gas mark 5
Use a 900g/2 lb loaf tin.

Grease and line the loaf tin. Sift the flour, baking powder, bicarb. and salt into a bowl and add the cinnamon. Rub in the butter until the mixture resembles fine breadcrumbs. Stir in the sugar, and make a well in the centre. Add the sour cream and milk and gradually draw in the dry ingredients to form a smooth dough.

Using floured hands shape the mixture into sixteen even-sized rounds. Place eight in the base of the tin. Sprinkle over half of the nuts and all of the prunes. Arrange the remaining dough rounds on top and sprinkle over the remaining chopped walnuts.

Bake in the oven for about 50 minutes or until firm to the touch. Check near the end of cooking time and cover with greaseproof paper if it is overbrowning. Turn out on to a wire rack and leave to cool for 1 hour. When cold brush with the honey to glaze.

Soft Fruit Loaf

FOR THE LOAF

METRIC	IMP.	US.	
450g	1 lb	4 cups	white self-raising flour
2 tsp.	2 tsp.	2 tsp.	baking powder
450g	1 lb	2 cups	cottage cheese
4 tbs.	4 tbs.	4 tbs.	sour cream
175g	6 oz	¾ cup	brown sugar
1 tbs.	1 tbs.	1 tbs.	vanilla sugar
pinch.	pinch.	pinch.	of salt
1 tbs.	1 tbs.	1 tbs.	grated lemon rind
1 tbs.	1 tbs.	1 tbs.	chopped almonds
1 tbs.	1 tbs.	1 tbs.	raisins
2 tbs.	2 tbs.	2 tbs.	chopped mixed candied fruit
2 tbs.	2 tbs.	2 tbs.	chopped mixed peel

TOPPING

METRIC	IMP.	US.	
1 tbs.	1 tbs.	1 tbs.	butter, melted
1 tbs.	1 tbs.	1 tbs.	icing sugar
1 tbs.	1 tbs.	1 tbs.	vanilla sugar

Preheat the oven to 190°C/375°F/Gas mark 5
Use a 1.4kg/3 lb loaf tin.

Grease and line the loaf tin. Press the cottage cheese through a sieve or liquidise. Sift the flour with the baking powder on to a pastry board and form a well in the centre. Add the cottage cheese, sour cream, sugar, vanilla sugar, salt, lemon rind, nuts, fruit and peel. Mix to a firm dough, knead lightly. Place in the loaf tin and bake for 50-60 minutes. leave to firm up in the tin before transferring the loaf to a wire cooling rack. Brush with melted butter while still hot. Mix the icing sugar and vanilla sugar and sift over the loaf.

Yorkshire Fruit Loaf

METRIC	IMP.	US.	
800g	1 ¾ lb	7 cups	white self-raising white flour
2 tsp.	2 tsp.	2 tsp.	baking powder
450g	1 lb	2 ½ cups	small currants
450g	1 lb	2 ½ cups	sultanas
350g	12 oz	1 ½ cup	butter
450g	1 lb	2 cups	dark soft brown sugar
6 tbs.	6 tbs.	6 tbs.	sour cream
600ml	1 pint	2 ½ cups	milk
175g	6 oz	1 cup	candied peel, finely chopped
50g	2 oz	¼ cup	chopped glacé cherries
1 tbs.	1 tbs.	1 tbs.	golden syrup
			grated rind of 1 lemon

Preheat the oven to 150°C/300°F/Gas mark 2
Use three 900g/2 lb loaf tins

Put the currants and sultanas into a bowl and cover with hot water. Steep until cold. Squeeze out the water and spread the fruit in the bottom of a large tin. Leave to dry overnight in a warm place.

Grease and line the base and sides of the loaf tins. Sift the flour and baking powder into a very large mixing bowl. Rub in the butter with the tips of your fingers and then stir in the sugar. Mix in the sour cream, fruit and enough milk to give a soft dropping consistency. Stir in the peel, cherries, syrup and lemon rind. Dissolve the bicarb. in a little of the milk and stir this into the mixture. Add enough of the remaining milk to achieve a soft but not sloppy consistency - you may not need all of it. Pour the mixture into the tins and weigh them to ensure it is evenly divided.

Bake for about 2 hours, or until the loaves are firm to the touch and beginning to shrink from the sides of the tins. Turn out and cool on wire trays. Peel off the lining papers and wrap each loaf tightly in foil or cling film

Sugar-Free Fruit Cake

METRIC	IMP.	US.	
225g	8 oz	2 cups	wholemeal self-raising flour
1 tsp.	1 tsp.	1 tsp.	baking powder
1 tsp.	1 tsp.	1 tsp.	mixed spices
1 tbs.	1 tbs.	1 tbs.	malt extract
225g	8 oz	1 cup	mixed dried fruit
100g	4 oz	½ cup	corn oil
125ml	8 tbs.	½ cup	yoghurt
			juice of ½ lemon

Preheat the oven to 160°C/325°F/Gas mark 3
Use a 15cm/6 inch square cake tin.

Oil the tin. Simmer the fruit with the spices and malt for approx. 10 minutes, making sure to keep the fruit well covered with water to stop it boiling dry. Leave to cool. Strain the cooled fruit and keep the liquid. Rub the oil, flour and baking powder together. Add the fruit and lemon juice.

Add the yoghurt to the mixture and enough water from stewing the fruit to make a dropping consistency. The stiffer the mixture, the drier the cake will be. Make sure the mixture is soft and drops from the spoon readily. Put the mixture into the tin. Bake in the pre-heated oven for 50 mins. Leave to cool in the tin.

Palm Sunday Fig Cake

METRIC	IMP.	US.	
225g	8 oz	2 cups	white self-raising flour
175g	6 oz	1 cup	dried figs
pinch.	pinch.	pinch.	of salt
6 tbs.	6 tbs.	6 tbs.	caster sugar
6 tbs.	6 tbs.	6 tbs.	butter

Preheat the oven to 190°C/375°F/Gas mark 5
Use an 18cm/7 inch cake tin.

Grease and flour the cake tin. Chop the figs and simmer in just enough water to cover them, until they are tender. Leave to cool. Mix together the flour, baking powder, salt and sugar. Rub in the butter. Mix to a batter with the cooled figs and cooking water. Pour into the cake tin, and bake for forty-five minutes.

Apricot Fruit Loaf

METRIC	*IMP.*	*US.*	
175g	6 oz	1 ½ cups	white self-raising flour
4 tbs.	4 tbs.	4 tbs.	sour cream
6 tbs.	6 tbs.	6 tbs.	butter
6 tbs.	6 tbs.	6 tbs.	light muscovado sugar
50g	2 oz	¼ cup	glacé cherries, quartered
75g	3 oz	½ cup	apricot pieces, chopped
75g	3 oz	½ cup	sultanas
125ml	8 tbs.	½ cup	milk

Preheat the oven to 160°C/325°F/Gas mark 3
Use a 450g/1 lb loaf tin.

Grease and line the loaf tin. Put the sour cream into a large bowl. Add all the other ingredients and beat well until smooth. Turn into the tin and level the top. Bake for about an hour until golden brown, firm to the touch and shrinking away from the sides of the tin. Test with a warm knife. Leave to cool in the tin.

Tutti-Frutti Cake.

FOR THE CAKE

METRIC	IMP.	US.	
225g	8 oz	2 cups	white self-raising flour
100g	4 oz	½ cup	butter
100g	4 oz	1 cup	caster sugar
125ml	8 tbs.	½ cup	sour cream
			grated rind of 1 large lemon

CREAM CHEESE FILLING AND DECORATION

METRIC	IMP.	US.	
225g	8 oz	1 cup	cream cheese
125ml	8 tbs.	½ cup	whipping cream
50g	2 oz	½ cup	icing sugar
2 tbs.	2 tbs.	2 tbs.	orange juice
2 tbs.	2 tbs.	2 tbs.	mixed glacé fruit, chopped finely

FOR THE ICING

METRIC	IMP.	US.	
225g	8 oz	1 ¼ cups	carob chips
1 tsp.	1 tsp.	1 tsp.	strong decaffeinated coffee
175g	6 oz	¾ cup	butter
4	4	4	mixed coloured glacé cherries, quartered

Preheat the oven to 160°C/325°F/Gas mark 3
Use a 450g/1 lb loaf tin.

Grease and line the loaf tin. Beat the butter and sugar together until light and creamy. Add the sour cream and beat thoroughly. Fold in the sieved flour, and then the lemon rind. Mix thoroughly. Turn the mixture into the tin and bake for 50-60 minutes, until well risen and nicely browned. Leave ten minutes to firm up , then turn out and cool on a wire tray.

Filling. Cut the cake into three even layers. Make the filling by beating the cream cheese with 1 tbs. of cream, the icing sugar and the juice, until it is quite smooth. Spread this over two layers, sprinkle with chopped glacé fruit and sandwich the cake back together again. Lift on to an oblong plate.

Icing. Melt the carob for the icing with the coffee, butter and 2 tbs. of water, stirring slowly until smooth. Allow to cool before beating in the remaining cream so that it is thick enough to coat the cake. Chill if necessary to speed up the process. Place a third of the icing in the piping bag, spread the remainder neatly over the cake. Pipe a small border round the base and top of the cake, using the smaller pipe. Lightly whip the remaining cream and then pipe slightly larger whirls, using the larger pipe. Place a piece of cherry on each whirl.

Date and Raisin Tea Bread

METRIC	IMP.	US.	
225g	8 oz	2 cups	white self-raising flour
½ tsp.	½ tsp.	½ tsp.	baking powder
100g	4 oz	½ cup	butter
75g	3 oz	½ cup	stoned dates, chopped
75g	3 oz	½ cup	walnut halves ,chopped
75g	3 oz	½ cup	seedless raisins
100g	4 oz	½ cup	demarara sugar
125ml	8 tbs.	½ cup	milk

Preheat the oven to 180°C/350°F/Gas mark 4
Use a 900g/2 lb loaf tin.

Grease and line the loaf tin with greaseproof paper. Sift together the flour and baking powder. Rub in the butter until the mixture resembles fine breadcrumbs. Stir in the dates, walnuts, raisins and sugar. Pour the milk into the centre of the dry ingredients. Mix well together to give a stiff dropping consistency, adding a little extra milk if necessary. Turn the mixture into the prepared tin and bake in the oven for about 1 hour, until well risen and just firm to the touch. Leave to firm up in the tin for ten minutes, before turning out to cool on a wire rack.

Country Tea Bread

METRIC	IMP.	US.	
225g	8 oz	2 cups	white self-raising flour
½ tsp.	½ tsp.	½ tsp.	baking powder
175g	6 oz	1 cup	sultanas
75g	3 oz	½ cup	currants
50g	2 oz	¼ cup	chopped glacé cherries
5 tbs.	5 tbs.	5 tbs.	golden syrup
125ml	8 tbs.	½ cup	cold rose hip tea (not too st
6 tbs.	6 tbs.	6 tbs.	sour cream
2 tbs.	2 tbs.	2 tbs.	butter, melted
2 tbs.	2 tbs.	2 tbs.	demerara sugar
25g	1 oz	¼ cup	walnuts, chopped

Preheat the oven to 180°C/350°F/Gas mark 4
Use a 450g/1 lb loaf tin.

Place the fruit in a large mixing bowl, pour in 4 tbs. of golden syrup and the cold tea and leave overnight. Next day, fold in the sour cream, sifted flour and melted butter.

Grease and line the loaf tin. Spoon the mixture into the tin and bake for about 50 minutes. Remove from the oven, brush the top with the remaining golden syrup and sprinkle on the sugar and walnuts. Return the loaf to the oven and bake for a further 15 minutes. Leave to firm up in the tin for 5 minutes then turn out onto a wire tray, peel off the lining paper and allow to cool.

A WALK IN THE AFRICAN NIGHT

CAKES WITH NUTS.

One of Srila Prabhupada's mottoes was 'Utility is the principle'. He worked hard and brought the Hare Krishna tradition out of India for the first time. He established the teachings throughout the world, and taught his followers a real determination to please Lord Krishna.

In the early days of the movement resources were scarce, yet the mission had to go on. There were no large temples with thousands of supporters, or great kitchens laden with fruit and vegetables. There were no warehouses full of books giving the message of Lord Krishna.

I had the great fortune to see Srila Prabhupada in 1975 at the Durban City Hall. He had a few full-time followers in South Africa, who by 1978 had organised a programme of visiting communities around the country with a marquee tent.

I was very excited when the tent came to Tongaat, our local town. My whole family walked four miles from our farm to the football ground where the festival was being held. We joined in the singing of the Hare Krishna mantra, we were absorbed by the dramatisation of the scriptures, staged by the devotees, and we listened intently to the lecture about spiritual life.

It was traditional at such events, to distribute prasadam or sanctified food, to all who took part. In India, a wealthy patron would sometimes pay for a sumptuous feast for thousands. I stood in line with my family to accept what the devotees had to offer.

After some time, we reached the head of the queue to receive a handful of nuts from Partha Sarathi, who has carried on the tent programme to this day. We eagerly accepted the nut prasadam, and set off through the bush in the hot African night, relishing the prasadam and the discussing the uplifting event.

Akinchana.

Pecan Sour Cream Cake

METRIC	IMP.	US.	
225g	8 oz	2 cups	white self-raising flour
1 tsp.	1 tsp.	1 tsp.	baking powder
½ tsp.	½ tsp.	½ tsp.	ground cinnamon
100g	4 oz	½ cup	butter
1 tsp.	1 tsp.	1 tsp.	vanilla essence
100g	4 oz	½ cup	caster sugar
300ml	½ pint	1 ¼ cups	sour cream
75g	3 oz	¾ cup	finely chopped pecan nuts
2 tbs.	2 tbs.	2 tbs.	brown sugar

Preheat the oven to 180°C/350°F/Gas mark 4
Use a deep 23cm/9 inch round cake tin.

Grease and line the loaf tin. Cream the butter, vanilla and caster sugar in small bowl until light and fluffy. Add 4 tbs. of sour cream and mix well. Transfer the mixture to large bowl. Stir in the remaining sour cream then the sifted flour and baking powder.

Spread half the cake mixture into the prepared tin. Sprinkle with half the combined pecans, brown sugar and cinnamon. Spread evenly with the remaining cake mixture. Sprinkle with the remaining pecan mixture, pressing gently into the cake mixture. Bake for about 1 hour. Stand 5 minutes before turning on to wire rack to cool.

Almond and Apricot Cake (Vegan)

METRIC	IMP.	US.	
150g	5 oz	1 ¼ cups	wholemeal self-raising flour
½ tsp.	½ tsp.	½ tsp.	baking powder
175g	6 oz	1 cup	dried apricots
300ml	½ pint	1 ¼ cups	soya milk
150g	5 oz	1 ¼ cups	chopped almonds
100g	4 oz	1 cup	ground almonds
175g	6 oz	¾ cup	vegetable margarine
100g	4 oz	½ cup	brown sugar
1 tsp.	1 tsp.	1 tsp.	almond essence
			a few whole almonds for decoration (optional)

Preheat the oven to 220°C/425°F/Gas mark 7
Use a 15cm/6 inch round cake tin.

Finely chop the apricots, put them in a bowl, pour the soya milk over, cover and leave to stand overnight.

Grease and line the cake tin. Sprinkle the chopped almonds on an oven proof plate and put them in the top of a hot oven till they begin to brown (about 8-12 minutes). Remove from the oven and set aside. Leave the oven door open and reduce heat to warm (325F/163C/gas mark 3) Put the flour, ground almonds and baking powder in a bowl and mix thoroughly. Melt the margarine and sugar in a small saucepan over a low heat before adding it to the flour mixture. Mix well and add the soaked apricots (together with any remaining liquid), the roasted almonds and the almond essence. Combine all the ingredients together thoroughly.

Transfer the mixture to a greased, floured cake tin, decorate with whole almonds and bake in the middle of a warm oven for about 50 minutes till a warm knife inserted in the centre comes out cleanly. Allow to cool in the tin before removing.

Hazelnut Cake

FOR THE CAKE

METRIC	IMP.	US.	
175g	6 oz	1 ½ cups	white self-raising flour
¼ tsp.	¼ tsp.	¼ tsp.	salt
100g	4 oz	½ cup	butter
175g	6 oz	¾ cup	caster sugar
1 tsp.	1 tsp.	1 tsp.	vanilla essence
125ml	8 tbs.	½ cup	milk
2 tbs.	2 tbs.	2 tbs.	sour cream
50g	2 oz	½ cup	ground hazelnuts

ICING:

METRIC	IMP.	US.	
175g	6 oz	1 ½ cups	icing sugar
1 tbs.	1 tbs.	1 tbs.	butter
1 tsp.	1 tsp.	1 tsp.	vanilla essence
1 tbs.	1 tbs.	1 tbs.	strong black decaff. coffee
25g	1 oz	¼ cup	chopped, toasted hazelnuts to decorate

Preheat the oven to 180°C/350°F/Gas mark 4
Use a 20cm/8 inch square cake tin.

Grease and flour the cake tin. Cream the butter and sugar together until light and fluffy. Add vanilla essence, sour cream and milk and mix until well combined. Fold in the flour and ground hazelnuts. Pour into the prepared tin and bake for 45 to 50 minutes or until a warm knife inserted in the middle comes out clean. Cool completely in the tin before removing.

Icing. Beat the ingredients together until smooth. Spread over the cake and sprinkle with chopped, toasted hazelnuts.

Walnut and Cherry Teabread

METRIC	IMP.	US.	
350g	12 oz	3 cups	white self-raising flour
1 tsp.	1 tsp.	1 tsp.	baking powder
1 tsp.	1 tsp.	1 tsp.	ground allspice
1 tsp.	1 tsp.	1 tsp.	ground cinnamon
75g	3 oz	½ cup	dates stoned and chopped
50g	2 oz	½ cup	chopped walnuts
300ml	½ pint	1 ¼ cups	milk
4 tbs.	4 tbs.	4 tbs.	golden syrup
100g	4 oz	½ cup	butter
100g	4 oz	½ cup	glacé cherries halved
6	6	6	walnut halves

Preheat the oven to 180°C/350°F/Gas mark 4
Use a 900g/2 lb loaf tin.

Grease and line the loaf tin. Sift the flour, baking powder and spices in a bowl and stir in dates and walnuts. Put the milk, syrup and butter in a saucepan and heat gently until melted, then mix to dry ingredients. Turn into the prepared tin, level the surface and arrange the cherries and walnuts on top. Bake for 1 to 1 and ¼ hours. Cut when completely cool.

Greek Walnut Cake

FOR THE CAKE

METRIC	IMP.	US.	
175g	6 oz	1 ½ cups	white self-raising flour
100g	4 oz	½ cup	butter
100g	4 oz	½ cup	sugar
4 tbs.	4 tbs.	4 tbs.	sour cream
1 tsp.	1 tsp.	1 tsp.	ground cinnamon
pinch.	pinch.	pinch.	of salt
175g	6 oz	1 ¾ cups	walnuts, finely chopped
125ml	8 tbs.	½ cup	milk

SYRUP

METRIC	IMP.	US.	
175g	6 oz	¾ cup	sugar
2.5cm	1 inch	1 inch	piece cinnamon stick
1 tbs.	1 tbs.	1 tbs.	lemon juice

Preheat the oven to 180°C/350°F/Gas mark 4
Use a 30 x 22.5cm/12 x 9 inch baking tin.

Cream together the butter and sugar until light and fluffy. Add the sour cream and beat until smooth. Sift together the flour, cinnamon and salt and fold into the mixture. Add milk. Now fold in the chopped walnuts.

Grease and flour the baking tin and spoon in the mixture. Smooth over the surface with the back of a spoon. Place in the oven and bake for 30-40 minutes or until cooked.

Syrup. Place the sugar, cinnamon stick, lemon juice and 450ml (¾ pint) water in a small saucepan and bring to the boil. Lower the heat and simmer for 10 minutes. Discard the cinnamon stick, and set aside to cool. When the cake is cooked remove from the oven. Pour the cool syrup evenly over the surface and leave in the tin until cold. Cut into squares or diamond-shaped pieces and serve with cream.

Balmoral Almond Cake

FOR THE CAKE

METRIC	IMP.	US.	
175g	6 oz	1 ½ cups	white self-raising flour
6 tbs.	6 tbs.	6 tbs.	butter
6 tbs.	6 tbs.	6 tbs.	caster sugar
4 tbs.	4 tbs.	4 tbs.	sour cream
50g	2 oz	½ cup	ground almonds
125ml	8 tbs.	½ cup	milk
			almond essence

FOR THE ICING AND DECORATION

METRIC	IMP.	US.	
4 tbs.	4 tbs.	4 tbs.	butter
100g	4 oz	1 cup	icing sugar
			almond essence
			toasted flaked almonds,
			icing sugar, for dredging

Preheat the oven to 160°C/325°F/Gas mark 3

A Balmoral cake tin is a ribbed loaf-shaped tin about 25.5 cm (10 inches) long, and is available from specialist kitchen shops. If you don't own one, use a 900 ml (1 ½ pint) loaf tin instead.

Grease the tin. Cream together the butter and the caster sugar until light and fluffy. Add a few drops of almond essence. Beat in the sour cream a little at a time. Fold in the ground almonds and flour with the milk. Spoon into the prepared tin and bake in the oven for 45-50 minutes or until risen and firm to the touch. Turn out on to a wire rack to cool.

Icing: To make the icing, cream the butter and icing sugar together and flavour with one or two drops of almond essence. Pipe down the centre of the cake, decorate with the almonds and dust lightly with icing sugar.

Maple Nut Cake (Vegan)

METRIC	IMP.	US.	
175g	6 oz	1 ½ cups	white self-raising flour
100g	4 oz	½ cup	caster sugar
2 tbs.	2 tbs	2 tbs.	maple syrup
75g	3 oz	½ cup	chopped pecans
125ml	8 tbs.	½ cup	vegetable oil
1 tsp.	1 tsp.	1 tsp.	lemon juice
125ml	8 tbs.	½ cup	water

Preheat the oven to 180°C/350°F/Gas mark 4
Use a 20cm/8 inch square cake tin.

Grease and line the cake tin. Mix the flour, sugar, baking powder, salt and pecans thoroughly. Stir in the remaining ingredients and mix well. Pour into the cake tin and bake for 35 to 40 minutes or until a warm knife inserted in the centre comes out clean.

Almond Cake

METRIC	IMP.	US.	
275g	10 oz	2 ½ cups	white self-raising flour
1 tsp.	1 tsp.	1 tsp.	baking powder
100g	4 oz	½ cup	caster sugar
100g	4 oz	½ cup	butter
6 tbs.	6 tbs.	6 tbs.	sour cream
250ml	8 fl. oz	1 cup	milk
½ tsp.	½ tsp.	½ tsp.	almond essence
50g	2 oz	½ cup	flaked almonds

Preheat the oven to 160°C/325°F/Gas mark 3
Use a 15cm/6 inch cake tin.

Grease and line the cake tin. In a mixing bowl, cream the butter with the sugar until light and fluffy. Sift together the flour and baking powder. In a jug beat the sour cream with the milk.

Add the dry ingredients to the creamed mixture in 3 parts, alternately with the sour cream and milk mixture. Beat well after each addition. Lightly stir in the almond essence and the flaked almonds. Spoon lightly into the prepared tin and bake for 1 ¼ to 1 ½ hours until cooked through and firm to the touch. Cool on a wire rack.

Walnut Buttermilk Loaf

METRIC	IMP.	US.	
275g	10 oz	2 ½ cups	white self-raising flour
2 tsp.	2 tsp.	2 tsp.	baking powder
50g	2 oz	½ cup	oatmeal
300ml	½ pint	1 ¼ cups	buttermilk
½ tsp.	½ tsp.	½ tsp.	salt
2 tsp.	2 tsp.	2 tsp.	grated orange rind
175g	6 oz	¾ cup	brown sugar
100g	4 oz	1 cup	chopped walnuts
2 tbs.	2 tbs.	2 tbs.	sour cream
1 tsp.	1 tsp.	1 tsp.	vanilla essence
5 tbs.	5 tbs.	5 tbs.	melted butter

Preheat the oven to 180°C/350°F/Gas mark 4
Use a 450g/1 lb loaf tin.

Combine the sour cream, buttermilk, vanilla, orange rind and melted butter. Sift together the dry ingredients, make a well in the centre and add the liquids. Mix lightly. Bake for 1 hour or until the cake shrinks away from the side of the tin. Leave to firm up in the tin for ten minutes. Turn out onto a wire rack to cool completely.

Peanut Butter Cake

FOR THE CAKE

METRIC	IMP.	US.	
225g	8 oz	2 cups	white self-raising flour
1 tsp.	1 tsp.	1 tsp.	baking powder
¼ tsp.	¼ tsp.	¼ tsp.	salt
100g	4 oz	½ cup	caster sugar
100g	4 oz	½ cup	butter, softened
1 tsp.	1 tsp.	1 tsp.	vanilla essence
6 tbs.	6 tbs.	6 tbs.	smooth peanut butter
4 tbs.	4 tbs.	4 tbs.	sour cream
125ml	8 tbs.	½ cup	milk

FILLING AND ICING

METRIC	IMP.	US.	
100g	4 oz	½ cup	butter, softened
100g	4 oz	½ cup	crunchy peanut butter
1 tsp.	1 tsp.	1 tsp.	vanilla essence
125ml	8 tbs.	½ cup	evaporated milk
350g	12 oz	3 cups	icing sugar
2 tbs.	2 tbs.	2 tbs.	carob powder

Preheat the oven to 180°C/350°F/Gas mark 4
Use two 20cm/8 inch sandwich tins.

Grease and line the sandwich tins. Beat the butter and sugar until creamy. Add the vanilla essence and peanut butter and beat well. Beat in the sour cream. Sift the flour, baking powder and salt together. Add to the butter-sugar-sour cream mixture by sifting and folding in alternate batches of the flour and the milk, about a third of each at a time. Mix lightly but thoroughly. Spoon the mixture into the sandwich tins.

Bake for 25 to 30 minutes. Remove from the oven and allow to stand for 2 to 3 minutes before turning out onto cake racks to cool. When cold, slice each cake in half horizontally, to make four layers.

Filing and Icing: Beat the butter, peanut butter and vanilla essence until creamy. Add the evaporated milk and beat thoroughly, then gradually add the sifted icing sugar and carob, beating until a soft spreading consistency is obtained.

Assembly: Use about two-thirds of the filling and icing mixture for filling. Spread the mixture between the four cake layers, re-forming the cake, and gently pressing to adhere. Spread the remaining mixture on top of the cake, swirling or roughing it to an attractive design. Chill before cutting, especially in warm weather.

Mrs Beeton's Almond Cake

METRIC	IMP.	US.	
275g	10 oz	2 ½ cups	white self-raising flour
1 tsp.	1 tsp.	1 tsp.	baking powder
100g	4 oz	½ cup	butter
100g	4 oz	½ cup	caster sugar
6 tbs.	6 tbs.	6 tbs.	sour cream
250ml	8 fl. oz	1 cup	milk
½ tsp.	½ tsp.	½ tsp.	almond essence
50g	2 oz	½ cup	flaked almonds
			butter for greasing

Preheat the oven to 160°C/325°F/Gas mark 3
Use a 15cm/6 inch cake tin.

Grease and line the cake tin. In a mixing bowl, cream the butter with the sugar until light and fluffy. Into another bowl, sift the flour and baking powder. In a measuring jug mix the sour cream with the milk. Add the dry ingredients to the creamed mixture in 3 parts, alternately with the sour cream and milk mixture. Beat well after each addition. Lightly stir in the almond essence and the flaked almonds. Spoon lightly into the prepared tin and bake for 1 ¼ to 1 ½ hours until cooked through and firm to the touch. Cool on a wire rack.

INDIA - LAND OF PLENTY.

MOIST AND RICH DRIED FRUIT CAKES

As a Hare Krishna follower, I was better prepared than most for my first visit to India. I felt at home as we landed at Delhi, and as we waited in the station for our train to Mathura, the birthplace of Krishna. After some weeks in Vrndavana, Krishna's childhood home and a visit to Bengal and Orissa, I returned to Delhi, on an early morning bus, with Kesava Bharati, senior preacher at the central London Hare Krishna temple.

We were bound for England the following day, and were both determined to finish off any last minute shopping as quickly as possible. We were looking for a particular brand of good quality incense. We made an unsuccessful visit to the air-conditioned shopping centre near Connaught Place in New Delhi, and set off by scooter taxi for Chandi Chowk in the older quarter of the city.

After transferring to a rickshaw in the midst of a chaotic traffic jam, we turned a corner into the bustle of Chandi Chowk. On both sides of the street, shops were laden with dried fruit of all descriptions. There were dates, raisins, figs, mangoes and guavas. Piles of cashews, groundnuts and dried coconut were displayed. Animated businessmen haggled over prices, and sacks were brought out and carried off on barrows.

India is portrayed as poor, yet the country is rich in natural produce. Markets are full of fresh vegetables and fruits. Every square metre of land is cultivated. There is little wastage. Many Indians are natural conservationists. Now the drive is on for industrialisation. Smoky factories form a grey belt around cities.

On returning to England, I watched a TV programme from Russia. Hundreds of people stood in a glum line for a few vegetables and a loaf of bread. The commentator spoke of the collapsing economy. India may be poor in foreign exchange and technical goods, but an economy based on the produce of the land will always be the most enduring.

Bhagavat.

Dried Fruit Cake

METRIC	IMP.	US.	
100g	4 oz	1 cup	white self-raising white flour
100g	4 oz	½ cup	butter, softened
100g	4 oz	½ cup	caster sugar
250ml.	8 fl. oz	1 cup	sour cream
5	5	5	dried dates, chopped
1 tbs.	1 tbs.	1 tbs.	pine-kernels
75g	3 oz	½ cup	seedless raisins
75g	3 oz	½ cup	dried apricots, chopped
100g	4 oz	¾ cup	carob chips
1 tbs.	1 tbs.	1 tbs.	vanilla essence
50g	2 oz	½ cup	hazelnuts, shelled and halved
50g	2 oz	½ cup	walnuts, shelled
			icing sugar for decoration

Preheat the oven to 180°C/350°F/Gas mark 4
Use a 900g/2 lb loaf tin.

In a large bowl, beat together the butter and sugar until light and fluffy. Add the sour cream beating well after addition. In a separate bowl mix the flour and dried fruit, then stir into the butter mixture. Add the carob chips, vanilla and nuts. Spoon into the loaf tin and bake for about 40 minutes. Remove from oven and leave to cool. When the cake is completely cooled sprinkle with icing sugar.

Boiled Apricot Fruit Cake

METRIC	IMP.	US.	
350g	12 oz	3 cups	white self-raising flour
250g	9 oz	1 ½ cups	chopped dried apricots
175g	6 oz	1 cup	chopped raisins
75g	3 oz	½ cup	chopped dates
175g	6 oz	¾ cup	glacé cherries
250g	9 oz	1 ½ cups	sultanas
75g	3 oz	½ cup	currants
175g	6 oz	1 cup	mixed peel
225g	8 oz	1 cup	butter
275g	10 oz	1 ¼ cups	light brown sugar
300ml	½ pint	1 ¼ cups	water
125ml	8 tbs.	½ cup	apple juice
75g	3 oz	¼ cup	apricot jam
6 tbs.	6 tbs.	6 tbs.	double cream, lightly beaten

Preheat the oven to 160°C/325°F/Gas mark 3
Use a deep 20cm/8 inch square cake tin.

Line and grease the cake tin. Combine the fruit, butter, sugar and water in saucepan. Stir constantly over the heat until the sugar is dissolved. Bring to the boil, reduce the heat, cover and simmer for 10 minutes. Remove from the heat. Stir in the apple juice and jam, cover, cool to room temperature. Stir the double cream, then the sifted flour into the fruit mixture. Mix well. Spread into the prepared tin. Bake for about 2 ½ hours. Cover with foil, cool in the tin.

Rich Fruit Cake

METRIC	IMP.	US.	
150g	5 oz	1 ¼ cups	white self-raising flour
75g	3 oz	½ cup	pitted prunes, halved
250g	9 oz	1 ½ cups	sultanas
250g	9 oz	1 ½ cups	currants
250ml.	8 fl. oz	1 cup	grape juice
125ml	8 tbs.	½ cup	apple juice
175g	6 oz	¾ cup	butter
100g	4 oz	½ cup	brown sugar
6 tbs.	6 tbs.	6 tbs.	sour cream
1 tbs.	1 tbs.	1 tbs.	dry instant decaff. coffee
5 tbs.	5 tbs.	5 tbs.	hot water
75g	3 oz	¼ cup	plum jam
1 tbs.	1 tbs.	1 tbs.	carob powder
1 tsp.	1 tsp.	1 tsp.	ground cinnamon
½ tsp.	½ tsp.	½ tsp.	mixed spice
½ tsp.	½ tsp.	½ tsp.	ground nutmeg
225g	8 oz	1 cup	glacé cherries
250g	9 oz	1 ½ cups	halved dates
175g	6 oz	1 cup	candied mixed peel
250g	9 oz	1 ½ cups	walnut pieces

Preheat the oven to 150°C/300°F/Gas mark 2
Use a deep 23cm/9 inch round cake tin.

Combine prunes, sultanas and currants in bowl, mix in grape juice and apple juice, cover, stand overnight. Grease and line the cake tin. Cream the butter and sugar in a small bowl until just combined. Add the sour cream and mix lightly. Transfer the mixture to large bowl. Stir in the combined coffee, water and jam, then the sifted dry ingredients in 2 lots. Drain the prune mixture, reserving the liquid. Add prune mixture, cherries, dates, peel and walnuts to the cake mixture. Mix well. Spread into the prepared tin. Bake for about 2 hours. Brush the reserved liquid over hot cake. Cover. Cool in the tin.

Texan Christmas Cake.

FOR THE CAKE

METRIC	IMP.	US.	
225g	8 oz	2 cups	white self-raising flour
pinch.	pinch.	pinch.	of salt
1 tsp.	1 tsp.	1 tsp.	mixed spice
½ tsp.	½ tsp.	½ tsp.	nutmeg
½ tsp.	½ tsp.	½ tsp.	cinnamon
225g	8 oz	1 cup	butter
225g	8 oz	1 cup	soft dark brown sugar
8 tbs.	8 tbs.	8 tbs.	sour cream
350g	12 oz	2 cups	raisins
100g	4 oz	½ cup	glacé cherries, chopped
225g	8 oz	1 cup	glacé pineapple, chopped
75g	3 oz	½ cup	dried apricots, chopped
175g	6 oz	1 ¾ cups	walnuts/pecan nuts, chopped
4 tbs.	4 tbs.	4 tbs.	honey
450ml	¾ pint	1 ¾ cups	milk

TO DECORATE:

METRIC	IMP.	US.	
2 tbs.	2 tbs.	2 tbs.	sieved apricot jam, warmed
			glacé cherries, halved
			whole mixed nuts (hazelnuts/pecan nuts)

Preheat the oven to 150°C/300°F/Gas mark 2
Use a 1.7 litre/3 pint ring tin.

Grease and line the ring tin. Sift together the flour, salt and spices. In a large mixing bowl, beat together the butter and sugar until light. Gradually add sour cream. Mix in the raisins, cherries, pineapple, apricots and nuts. Add the flour, alternately with the milk, and gently mix in until well blended. Spoon the mixture into the prepared tin and smooth the top.

Bake in the preheated oven for 1 ½ hours, then reduce the temperature to 140°C/275°F/Gas mark 1 for a further 2 to 2 ½ hours. Leave the cake to cool in the tin, then invert onto a wire rack. Skewer the cake evenly all over and spoon honey into the holes.

Decoration: Brush a little warmed jam over the top of the cake and arrange cherry halves and nuts on top. Brush with the remaining jam.

Lebanese Date Cake

METRIC	IMP.	US.	
225g	8 oz	2 cups	white self-raising flour
1 tsp.	1 tsp.	1 tsp.	salt
175g	6 oz	¾ cup	brown sugar
100g	4 oz	½ cup	unsalted butter
6 tbs.	6 tbs.	6 tbs.	sour cream
250ml	8 fl. oz	1 cup	milk
175g	6 oz	1 cup	dried dates, finely chopped
2 tbs.	2 tbs.	2 tbs.	pistachios, finely chopped
2 tbs.	2 tbs.	2 tbs.	raisins, chopped
½ tsp.	½ tsp.	½ tsp.	ground nutmeg
1 tsp.	1 tsp.	1 tsp.	vanilla essence

Preheat the oven to 180°C/350°F/Gas mark 4
Use a 20cm/8 inch round cake tin.

Grease and flour the cake tin. Sift the flour and salt into a large bowl. Stir in the sugar. Add the butter and rub in with your fingertips until the mixture resembles fine breadcrumbs. Fold in the sour cream and the milk. Stir in the remaining ingredients and mix until well blended.

Pour the cake mixture into the tin. Smooth over the surface with the back of a spoon. Bake for about 50-60 minutes or until the cake is cooked. Remove from the oven, cool in the tin and then turn out and leave on a rack until cold.

Boiled Fruit Cake (Vegan)

METRIC	IMP.	US.	
350g	12 oz	3 cups	white self-raising flour
300ml	½ pint	1 ¼ cups	freshly made apple juice
175g	6 oz	¾ cup	brown sugar
350g	12 oz	1 ½ cups	mixed dried fruit
100g	4 oz	½ cup	vegetable margarine
2 tsp.	2 tsp.	2 tsp.	mixed spice
½ tsp.	½ tsp.	½ tsp.	grated lemon rind

Preheat the oven to 160°C/325°F/Gas mark 3
Use an 18cm/7 inch cake tin.

Lightly grease and line the tin. Place the apple juice, fruit, sugar and margarine in a pan, bring to the boil. Reduce the heat and simmer for 10 mins. then cool. Sift the flour and spices and stir in. Add the lemon rind. Mix and pour into the tin. Bake for 1 hour, until risen and firm. Turn out on wire rack.

Moist Date Cake

METRIC	IMP.	US.	
225g	8 oz	2 cups	white self-raising flour
½ tsp.	½ tsp.	½ tsp.	baking powder
½ tsp.	½ tsp.	½ tsp.	bicarb.
250g	9 oz	1 ½ cups	dates
300ml	½ pint	1 ¼ cups	water
175g	6 oz	¾ cup	butter
175g	6 oz	¾ cup	caster sugar
6 tbs.	6 tbs.	6 tbs.	sour cream

Preheat the oven to 180°C/350°F/Gas mark 4
Use a deep 20cm/8 inch square cake tin.

Combine dates, water and soda in bowl, cover, stand overnight. Grease and line the base of the cake tin with paper. Grease the paper well.

Cream the butter and sugar in a small bowl until light and fluffy. Add sour cream and mix well. Transfer mixture to large bowl, stir in half the sifted flours and half the undrained date mixture, then stir in remaining flours and date mixture. Spread into the prepared tin. Bake for about 1 ¼ hours. Stand 5 minutes before turning on to wire rack to cool.

One-Stage Fruit Cake

METRIC	IMP.	US.	
225g	8 oz	2 cups	white self-raising flour
1 tsp.	1 tsp.	1 tsp.	mixed spice
100g	4 oz	½ cup	soft butter
100g	4 oz	½ cup	glacé cherries, chopped
75g	3 oz	½ cup	currants
75g	3 oz	½ cup	sultanas
2 tbs.	2 tbs.	2 tbs.	cut mixed peel
100g	4 oz	½ cup	soft light brown sugar
4 tbs.	4 tbs.	4 tbs.	sour cream
125ml.	4 fl. oz.	½ cup	milk
			butter for greasing

Preheat the oven to 180°C/350°F/Gas mark 4
Use an 18cm/7 inch round cake tin.

Grease and line the cake tin. Sift together the flour and mixed spice. Put all the ingredients in a bowl, stir, then beat until smooth. Spoon the mixture into the prepared tin and bake for 2 hours. Cool on a wire rack.

Vegan Celebration Cake

METRIC	IMP.	US.	
225g	8 oz	2 cups	wholemeal self-raising flour
250g	9 oz	1 ½ cups	sultanas
250g	9 oz	1 ½ cups	raisins
175g	6 oz	1 cup	currants
300ml	½ pint	1 ¼ cups	apple juice concentrate
175g	6 oz	¾ cup	vegetable margarine
6 tbs.	6 tbs.	6 tbs.	raw demerara sugar
3 tbs.	3 tbs.	3 tbs.	molasses
125ml	8 tbs.	½ cup	soya milk
2 tbs.	2 tbs.	2 tbs.	mixed spice

Preheat the oven to 150°C/300°F/Gas mark 2
Use a 23cm/9 inch round cake tin.

Put all the dried fruit in a bowl, pour the apple juice concentrate over and leave to soak overnight, Stir from time to time to make sure all the fruit is soaked.

Put the margarine and sugar in a large mixing-bowl and cream well together before stirring in the molasses, flour, soya milk and mixed spice. An electric mixer may be used if you prefer. Fold in the soaked dried fruit and stir till evenly distributed through the mixture.

Line the cake tin with grease-proof paper. Pour in the mixture and bake for about 3 hours till a warm knife inserted in the centre comes out cleanly. Allow to cool on a rack before removing from tin.

Dundee Cake

One of the great favourites. Be careful just to rest the almonds on top of the mixture before cooking so that they do not sink right into the cake mixture.

METRIC	IMP.	US.	
200g	7 oz	1 ¾ cups	white self-raising flour
175g	6 oz	¾ cup	soft butter
175g	6 oz	¾ cup	caster sugar
300ml	½ pint	1 ¼ cups	sour cream
1 tbs.	1 tbs.	1 tbs.	maple syrup
1 tbs.	1 tbs.	1 tbs.	lemon juice
3 tbs.	3 tbs.	3 tbs.	ground almonds
75g	3 oz	½ cup	mixed peel
75g	3 oz	½ cup	sultanas
75g	3 oz	½ cup	currants
75g	3 oz	½ cup	raisins
50g	2 oz	¼ cup	glacé cherries, quartered
3 tbs.	3 tbs.	3 tbs.	split blanched almonds for topping

Preheat the oven to 150°C/300°F/Gas mark 2
Use a 20cm/8 inch deep round cake tin.

Grease and line the cake tin. Measure the butter and sugar into a bowl and cream together until light and fluffy. Beat in the sour cream a little at a time together with 2 tbs. of the flour. Fold in the remaining flour with the remaining ingredients until evenly blended. Turn into the prepared tin and level the top.

Arrange the split almonds gently on top of the mixture then bake in the oven for about 2 ½ - 3 hours. Test that the cake with a warm knife inserted into the centre. If it comes out clean, the cake is cooked. Allow to cool in the tin for about 30 minutes, then turn out and finish cooling on a wire rack.

Christmas Cake (1)

FOR THE CAKE

METRIC	IMP.	US.	
200g	7 oz	1 ¾ cups	white self-raising flour
250g	9 oz	1 ½ cups	currants
175g	6 oz	1 cup	raisins
75g	3 oz	½ cup	sultanas
75g	3 oz	½ cup	dried apricots, finely chopped
75g	3 oz	¾ cup	flaked almonds
300ml	½ pint	1 ¼ cups	orange juice
175g	6 oz	¾ cup	soft unsalted butter
100g	4 oz	½ cup	caster sugar
2 tbs.	2 tbs.	2 tbs.	molasses
8 tbs.	8 tbs.	8 tbs.	sour cream
50g	2 oz	½ cup	ground almonds
1 tsp.	1 tsp.	1 tsp.	ground mixed spice
½ tsp.	½ tsp.	½ tsp.	ground cinnamon
¼ tsp.	¼ tsp.	¼ tsp.	ground nutmeg
3 tbs.	3 tbs.	3 tbs.	milk
			grated rind 1 lemon

DECORATION.

METRIC	IMP.	US.	
2 tbs.	2 tbs.	2 tbs.	apricot jam
2 tbs.	2 tbs.	2 tbs.	clear honey
2 tbs.	2 tbs.	2 tbs.	boiling water
			a selection of halved shelled nuts

Preheat the oven to 140°C/275°F/Gas mark 1
Use a 20cm/8 inch round cake tin.

Place the dried fruit in a bowl with the flaked almonds, lemon rind and orange juice, cover with a damp cloth and leave to stand for 8 hours or overnight.

Grease and line the base and sides of the cake tin with a double layer of greased greaseproof paper. Tie a thick band of brown paper around the outside of the tin and stand it on a pad of brown paper on a baking sheet to protect the cake during cooking.

Cream the butter, sugar and molasses together until light and fluffy. Gradually beat in the sour cream, a little at a time, adding the ground almonds alternately and mixing well after each addition.

Sieve the flour and spices into the bowl, adding any bran remaining in the sieve. Add the fruit, with the liquid, then the milk and mix to a dropping consistency. Spoon into the prepared tin and smooth the top. Cover the top loosely with several layers of greaseproof paper and a layer of brown paper.

Bake in the preheated cool oven. Check the cake after 2 ½ hours, and then at half hourly intervals. Test by inserting a warm knife into the centre of the cake; if it emerges clean then the cake is ready.

Remove from the oven and leave to cool in the tin until completely cold. Remove from tin, and take out of the lining paper.

Decoration: Arrange the nut halves on the top of the cake. Make a glaze by combining the apricot jam with the honey and boiling water in a small bowl. This makes a smooth, shiny paste. Brush this over the top of the cake.

Christmas Cake (2)

METRIC	IMP.	US.	
225g	8 oz	2 cups	white self-raising flour
225g	8 oz	1 cup	butter
225g	8 oz	1 cup	soft brown sugar
1 tsp.	1 tsp.	1 tsp.	ground mixed spice
½ tsp.	½ tsp.	½ tsp.	grated nutmeg
1 tbs.	1 tbs.	1 tbs.	golden syrup
450ml	¾ pint	1 ¾ cups	sour cream
75g	3 oz	¾ cup	ground almonds
350g	12 oz	2 cups	currants
250g	9 oz	1 ½ cups	sultanas
175g	6 oz	1 cup	raisins
100g	4 oz	½ cup	glacé cherries, quartered
75g	3 oz	½ cup	chopped mixed peel
50g	2 oz	½ cup	split almonds
			grated rind of 1 lemon

Preheat the oven to 150°C/300°F/Gas mark 2
Use a 23cm/9 inch square cake tin.

Line the base and sides of the cake tin with a double layer of greaseproof paper. Tie a thick band of brown paper around the outside of the tin and stand it on a pad of brown paper on a baking sheet. Sift flour and spice together. Cream butter, sugar and golden syrup together until light and fluffy. Add sour cream and mix well. Fold in flour, fruit and nuts until thoroughly mixed. Place in prepared tin, smooth the top. Bake for 3 to 4 hours, test with a warm knife after 3 hrs. Leave in tin for 20 minutes, then turn onto wire rack to cool.

Sienna Cake (Vegan)

A traditional Italian rich celebration cake, made without flour.

METRIC	IMP.	US.	
175g	6 oz	½ cup	golden syrup
100g	4 oz	½ cup	sugar
75g	3 oz	¾ cup	chopped hazelnuts
75g	3 oz	¾ cup	chopped walnuts
75g	3 oz	¾ cup	blanched, chopped walnuts
100g	4 oz	½ cup	glacé cherries chopped
1 tbs.	1 tbs.	1 tbs.	ground ginger
75g	3 oz	½ cup	pineapples chopped
75g	3 oz	½ cup	chopped, pressed dates
75g	3 oz	¾ cup	carob powder
½ tsp.	½ tsp.	½ tsp.	mace
½ tsp.	½ tsp.	½ tsp.	coriander
½ tsp.	½ tsp.	½ tsp.	mixed spice
			a little icing sugar

Preheat the oven to 150°C/300°F/Gas mark 2
Use a 23cm/9 inch loose bottom cake tin.

Grease the cake tin. Put the sugar and golden syrup into a heavy saucepan and stir over a gentle heat until dissolved. Bring to the boil and boil gently until the mixture reaches 'soft ball' stage - when syrup registers 114 deg. C. on a sugar thermometer.

Remove the pan from the heat and stir in the remaining ingredients, except the icing sugar. It will be quite stiff at this stage of preparation. Press the mixture into the prepared tin. Bake for 30 minutes. Lift the cake out on the loose bottom base of the tin and allow it to cool on a wire rack. Dredge with sifted icing sugar and serve cut into thin wedges.

Cream Cheese Fruit Cake

METRIC	IMP.	US.	
100g	4 oz	1 cup	white self-raising white flour
100g	4 oz	½ cup	butter
100g	4 oz	½ cup	cream cheese
2 tsp.	2 tsp.	2 tsp.	grated lemon rind
175g	6 oz	¾ cup	caster sugar
4 tbs.	4 tbs.	4 tbs.	sour cream
175g	6 oz	1 cup	sultanas
175g	6 oz	1 cup	chopped raisins
175g	6 oz	1 cup	currants
175g	6 oz	¾ cup	chopped glacé apricots
225g	8 oz	1 cup	quartered glacé cherries
250ml	8 fl. oz	1 cup	grape juice

Preheat the oven to 150°C/300°F/Gas mark 2
Use a deep 20cm/8 inch round cake tin.

Line the cake tin with 2 sheets of paper. Cream the butter, cream cheese, rind and sugar until light and fluffy. Add the sour cream and mix well. Transfer the mixture to large bowl, stir in fruit and grape juice then the sifted flours in 2 lots. Spread the mixture into prepared tin. Bake for about 1 ½ hours. Cover with foil and cool in the tin.

Date and Walnut Loaf

METRIC	IMP.	US.	
50g	2 oz	½ cup	white self-raising flour
250g	9 oz	1 ½ cups	chopped dates
125ml	8 tbs.	½ cup	strong rosehip tea
½ tsp.	½ tsp.	½ tsp.	bicarb.
175g	6 oz	¾ cup	butter
175g	6 oz	¾ cup	caster sugar
4 tbs.	4 tbs.	4 tbs.	sour cream
100g	4 oz	1 cup	chopped walnuts
2 tbs.	2 tbs.	2 tbs.	grape juice

Preheat the oven to 150°C/300°F/Gas mark 2
Use a 900g/2 lb loaf tin.

Combine dates, tea and soda in bowl; cover, stand overnight. Line the base and sides of the loaf tin with greaseproof paper. Grease the paper well. Cream the butter and sugar in small bowl until light and fluffy, add sour cream and mix well. Transfer to large bowl. Stir in walnuts, sifted flour and grape juice then date mixture. Pour into prepared tin. Bake for about 1 hour. Stand for 15 minutes before turning on to wire rack to cool.

Simnel Cake

METRIC	IMP.	US.	
225g	8 oz	2 cups	white self-raising flour
175g	6 oz	¾ cup	butter
175g	6 oz	¾ cup	caster sugar
125ml.	4 fl. oz.	½ cup	sour cream
450g	1 lb	2 ½ cups	raisins
50g	2 oz	¼ cup	glacé cherries, quartered
125ml	8 tbs.	½ cup	milk
2 tsp.	2 tsp.	2 tsp.	mixed spice
450g	1 lb	1 lb	marzipan

Preheat the oven to 160°C/325°F/Gas mark 3
Use a 20cm/8 inch deep round cake tin.

Grease the cake tin and line with greaseproof paper. In a large mixing bowl, beat together the butter and sugar until light and fluffy. Beat in the sour cream, a little at a time. Stir in the raisins and cherries, then the milk. Sift together the flour and spice and fold into the fruit mixture until evenly blended.

Roll out half the marzipan to a 20 cm/8 inch round. Place half the cake mixture in the prepared tin and cover with the round of marzipan. Spoon over the remaining cake mixture and smooth the surface. Bake for 2 ¼ hours, until the cake springs back. Leave to cool in the tin.

THE COSMIC POWER OF GINGER

CAKES WITH SPICES.

The missionary activities of the Hare Krishna movement involve the selling of books and chanting of the Hare Krishna mantra. In England, 13 million books written by Srila Prabhupada have sold. Devotees have gone out every day to chant on London's Oxford Street since 1969.

Both activities are described as sankirtan, or glorification of Lord Krishna, and often require some physical sacrifice. This is particularly true in the British winter. After initial training at Bhaktivedanta Manor, I rejoined my home temple at Leicester. It was early December. It was here that I encountered the legendary *brahmastra*.

After some weeks of distributing books and devotional pictures to the many Hindu households in the area, I developed a chest cold, and was forced to rest. Our cook, Gaura Purusha prescribed a *brahmastra* and set off for the kitchen to prepare it. My limited understanding of scripture told me that a *brahmastra* was a weapon which was used in classical Vedic times. It resembled a nuclear weapon, although it had a much more localised effect. I sat in the restaurant anticipating Gaura's return.

He emerged with a smile and handed me a cup of foaming liquid, which looked like something from Dr. Frankenstein's laboratory. I raised the cup to my lips, uttered a prayer and drank. Before I had put the cup back on the table, an atomic explosion went off in my stomach. My eyes streamed, my limbs began to glow and the room spun. Gaura explained that this traditional remedy was made with liberal quantities of ginger, chilli powder, mustard, cumin, coriander and tamarind. Whole red chillies are optional.

I was back out the next day, fully recovered. Ginger is a potent spice, good at stimulating the digestion and cleaning the blood.

Bhagavat.

Yasomati's Moist Ginger Cake

In the north of England lies the ancient cathedral city of Durham. Nearby, Hare Krishna devotees Laghu Hari and Yasomati raise their children and their vegetables, in a 13th century farmhouse, near the river Wear. This cake is Yasomati's speciality, which can be suitable for Vegan's if Soya milk is used. Pear and Apple spread is common in vegetarian and wholefood shops.

METRIC	IMP.	US.	
125g	5oz	1 ¼ cups	plain flour
225g	8oz	2 cups	wholemeal flour
225g	8oz	1 cup	pear and apple spread
300ml	1/2 pint	1 ¼ cups	milk
2 tsp.	2 tsp.	2 tsp.	lemon juice
100g	4oz	½ cup	vegetable margarine
4 tsp.	4 tsp.	4 tsp.	ground ginger
50g	2oz	¼ cup	stem ginger (3-4 pieces)
2 tsp.	2 tsp.	2 tsp.	bicarb.
2 tsp.	2 tsp.	2 tsp.	boiling water
			a few flaked almonds

Preheat the oven to 180°C/350°F/Gas mark 4
Use a 20 cm/8 inch square tin.

Grease and line the tin. Mix together the fruit spread, milk, lemon juice, margarine and spices in a pan. Heat gently until the margarine and spread are melted. Sift together the flours and ground ginger in a large bowl. Stir in the melted mixture. Dissolve the bicarb in the boiling water and add to the mixture. Beat well until evenly mixed. Pour into prepared tin. Sprinkle with flaked almonds and bake in the preheated oven for 30-45 minutes. Cool in tin. Cut in squares when completely cold.

Allspice Malt Ring.

FOR THE CAKE

METRIC	IMP.	US.	
225g	8 oz	2 cups	white self-raising flour
½ tsp.	½ tsp.	½ tsp.	baking powder
1 tsp.	1 tsp.	1 tsp.	ground allspice
¼ tsp.	¼ tsp.	¼ tsp.	bicarb.
50g	2 oz	½ cup	walnuts, chopped
75g	3 oz	½ cup	dried apricots, chopped
2 tbs.	2 tbs	2 tbs.	golden syrup
2 tbs.	2 tbs.	2 tbs.	malt extract
2 tbs.	2 tbs.	2 tbs.	brown sugar
125ml	8 tbs.	½ cup	milk

ICING AND DECORATION:

METRIC	IMP.	US.	
100g	4 oz	1 cup	icing sugar, sifted
2 tsp.	2 tsp.	2 tsp.	hot water (approximately)
50g	2 oz	¼ cup	glacé cherries, quartered

Preheat the oven to 160°C/325°F/Gas mark 3
Use a 20cm/8 inch ring tin.

Thoroughly grease and flour the ring tin. Sift the flour, allspice, baking powder and bicarb. together into a bowl. Stir in the walnuts and apricots. Warm the syrup, malt and sugar in a pan over low heat. Add the milk. Make a well in the centre of the dry ingredients and pour in the syrup mixture. Beat well to give a smooth, soft dropping consistency. Pour into the prepared tin and bake in the centre of the preheated oven for 1 - 1 ¼ hours or until golden brown and firm. Carefully turn out onto a wire rack to cool.

Icing and Decoration: Combine the icing sugar with enough hot water to give a thick, spreading consistency. Pour over the ring. Decorate with glacé cherries. Makes one 8 inch ring cake

Ginger and Carob Cake

FOR THE CAKE

METRIC	IMP.	US.	
225g	8 oz	2 cups	white self-raising flour
½ tsp.	½ tsp.	½ tsp.	baking powder
75g	3 oz	¼ cup	golden syrup
175g	6 oz	¾ cup	brown sugar, firmly packed
1 tbs.	1 tbs.	1 tbs.	ground ginger
225g	8 oz	1 cup	butter, melted
125ml	8 tbs.	½ cup	water

SYRUP CREAM

METRIC	IMP.	US.	
125ml	8 tbs.	½ cup	water
175g	6 oz	¾ cup	caster sugar
1 tbs.	1 tbs.	1 tbs.	golden syrup
175g	6 oz	¾ cup	butter
100g	4 oz	¾ cup	carob chips

Preheat the oven to 160°C/325°F/Gas mark 3
Use a 23cm/9 inch square slab tin.

Grease the cake tin. Mix all the cake ingredients in a large bowl until well combined. Beat for about 3 minutes or until mixture is changed in colour and smooth. Pour mixture into prepared tin. Bake for about 1 hour. Stand 5 minutes before turning on to wire rack to cool. Melt carob over hot water and cool, but do not allow to set. Spread cold cake with syrup Cream, drizzle with melted carob.

Syrup Cream: Combine water, sugar and syrup in saucepan, stir constantly over heat without boiling until sugar is dissolved. Bring to the boil, remove from heat. Cool to room temperature, allow to become completely cold. Beat the butter in a small bowl until white and fluffy. Gradually add syrup, beating well after each addition.

Cinnamon Ginger Cake

FOR THE CAKE

METRIC	IMP.	US.	
150g	5 oz	1 ¼ cups	white self-raising flour
6 tbs.	6 tbs.	6 tbs.	caster sugar
175g	6 oz	¾ cup	butter
2 tbs.	2 tbs.	2 tbs.	sour cream
75g	3 oz	¼ cup	golden syrup
2 tsp.	2 tsp.	2 tsp.	ground ginger
1 tsp.	1 tsp.	1 tsp.	ground cinnamon
5 tbs.	5 tbs.	5 tbs.	hot water

CARAMEL ICING

METRIC	IMP.	US.	
6 tbs.	6 tbs.	6 tbs.	butter
100g	4 oz	½ cup	brown sugar
2 tbs.	2 tbs.	2 tbs.	milk
175g	6 oz	1 ½ cups	icing sugar
1 tsp.	1 tsp.	1 tsp.	vanilla essence

Preheat the oven to 180°C/350°F/Gas mark 4
Use a deep 20cm/8 inch round cake tin.

Grease the tin. Cream the butter and sugar in a small bowl until light and fluffy. Add the sour cream. Mix well. Gradually add the syrup and beat well. Transfer the mixture to large bowl. Stir in half the sifted dry ingredients with half the water, then the remainder. Stir until smooth. Pour into the prepared tin. Bake for about 1 hour. Stand 5 minutes before turning on to wire rack to cool. Top the cold cake with icing. Sprinkle with a little extra cinnamon.

Caramel Icing: Combine the butter and sugar in a saucepan. Stir constantly over heat without boiling until the butter is melted and the sugar dissolved. Add the milk and stir for a further 2 minutes over the heat. Transfer the mixture to small bowl. Gradually beat in the sifted icing sugar and essence.

Golden Gingerb

METRIC	IMP.	US.	
200g	7 oz	1 ¾ cups	white self-raisir
½ tsp.	½ tsp.	½ tsp.	baking powder
¼ tsp.	¼ tsp.	¼ tsp.	salt
1 tbs.	1 tbs.	1 tbs.	ground ginger
6 tbs.	6 tbs.	6 tbs.	butter
4 tbs.	4 tbs.	4 tbs.	demarara sugar
175g	6 oz	½ cup	golden syrup
2 tbs.	2 tbs.	2 tbs.	sour cream
			butter for greasing
			grated rind of 1 orange
			milk

Preheat the oven to 160°C/325°F/Gas mark 3
Use a 15cm/6 inch square cake tin.

Grease and line the cake tin. Sift the flour, salt, ginger and baking powder into a mixing bowl. Stir in the orange rind. Warm the butter with the sugar and syrup in a saucepan until the butter has melted but the mixture is not hot.

In a measuring jug, whisk the sour cream and add enough milk to make up to 125ml/ 4 fl oz. Add the melted mixture to the dry ingredients with the whisked sour cream and milk mixture. Stir thoroughly. The mixture should run easily off the spoon. Pour into the prepared tin and bake for 1 ¼ - 1 ½ hours until firm. Cool on a wire rack.

Rich Gingerbread

METRIC	IMP.	US.	
225g	8 oz	2 cups	white self-raising flour
½ tsp.	½ tsp.	½ tsp.	baking powder
¼ tsp.	¼ tsp.	¼ tsp.	salt
2 tsp.	2 tsp.	2 tsp.	ground ginger
1 tsp.	1 tsp.	1 tsp.	ground cinnamon
100g	4 oz	½ cup	butter
100g	4 oz	½ cup	soft light brown sugar
175g	6 oz	½ cup	golden syrup
2 tbs.	2 tbs.	2 tbs.	sour cream
125ml	8 tbs.	½ cup	plain yoghurt
2 tbs.	2 tbs.	2 tbs.	ginger preserve
			butter for greasing

Preheat the oven to 160°C/325°F/Gas mark 3
Use a 23cm/9 inch square cake tin.

Grease and line the cake tin. Sift the flour, salt, spices and baking powder into a mixing bowl. Heat the butter, sugar and syrup in a saucepan until the butter has melted. In a bowl, whisk the sour cream and yoghurt together. Add to the dry ingredients, with the melted mixture, to give a soft, dropping consistency. Stir in the preserve. Spoon into the prepared tin and bake for 50-60 minutes until cooked through and firm to the touch. Cool on a wire rack.

Vegan Spice Cake.

METRIC	IMP.	US.	
350g	12 oz	3 cups	wholemeal flour
100g	4 oz	½ cup	vegetable oil
175g	6 oz	1 ½ cups	sugar
1 tsp.	1 tsp.	1 tsp.	bicarb.
1 tsp.	1 tsp.	1 tsp.	ground cloves
1 tsp.	1 tsp.	1 tsp.	ground cinnamon
75g	3 oz	½ cup	currants
25g	1 oz	¼ cup	walnut pieces
			juice of 2 oranges
125ml	4 fl. oz	½ cup	water

Preheat the oven to 200°C/400°C/Gas mark 6.
Use a 450g/1 lb loaf tin.

Grease and line the loaf tin. Place all the ingredients except the flour in a large bowl and mix well Fold in the flour. Meanwhile, add the bicarb to the orange juice. Pour the orange and bicarb. mixture into the mixing bowl and stir thoroughly. Spoon the contents of the bowl into the loaf tin. Place in the preheated oven and bake for 1 hour, or until a clean knife inserted in the centre comes out clean. Cool in the tin for ten minutes, then turn out onto a wire rack.

Dark Ginger Cake

METRIC	IMP.	US.	
225g	8 oz	2 cups	wholemeal self-raising flour
1 tsp.	1 tsp.	1 tsp.	baking powder
1 tbs.	1 tbs.	1 tbs.	ground ginger
1 tsp.	1 tsp.	1 tsp.	mustard powder
1 tsp	1 tsp	1 tsp	ground cinnamon
250ml	8 fl. oz	1 cup	sunflower oil
5 tbs.	5 tbs.	5 tbs.	molasses
5 tbs.	5 tbs.	5 tbs.	malt extract
3 tbs.	3 tbs.	3 tbs.	golden syrup
4 tbs.	4 tbs.	4 tbs.	sour cream
125ml	8 tbs.	½ cup	skimmed milk

Preheat the oven to 150°C/300°F/Gas mark 2
Use a 900g/2 lb loaf tin.

Base line and grease the loaf tin. Mix together the flour, ginger, mustard powder, cinnamon and baking powder, then set aside. In another bowl, beat together the oil, molasses, malt extract, syrup, sour cream and milk. Fold the dry ingredients into the beaten mixture.

Pour into the prepared tin and bake on the bottom shelf of the preheated oven for 1 ¼ - 1 ½ hours, or until a warm knife inserted into the cake comes out clean. Turn out on to a wire rack and leave until completely cold before removing the lining paper.

Iced Ginger Cake (Ve

FOR THE CAKE

METRIC	IMP.	US.	
350g	12 oz	3 cups	white self-raising flour
1 tsp.	1 tsp.	1 tsp.	baking powder
225g	8 oz	1 cup	dark soft brown sugar
4 tbs.	4 tbs.	4 tbs.	soya milk
250ml	8 fl. oz	1 cup	corn oil
175g	6 oz	½ cup	golden syrup
250ml	8 fl. oz	1 cup	hot water
2 tsp.	2 tsp.	2 tsp.	ground ginger
½ tsp.	½ tsp.	½ tsp.	ground mixed spice
100g	4 oz	½ cup	glacé ginger, finely chopped

DECORATION

METRIC	IMP.	US.	
150g	5 oz	1 ¼ cup	icing sugar, sifted
2 tbs.	2 tbs.	2 tbs.	hot water
2tbs.	2 tbs.	2 tbs.	crystallised ginger

Preheat the oven to 150°C/300°F/Gas mark 2
Use a 33 x 25cm/13 x 10 inch cake tin.

Grease and line the cake tin. Whisk the sugar and soya milk together. Beat in the oil and syrup, then fold in the flour and baking powder. Add the ground ginger to the creamed mixture, with the mixed spice and chopped glacé ginger. Pour the mixture into the prepared tin. Bake in the preheated oven at for about 1 hour until well risen and firm to the touch. Allow the cake to cool in the tin. When cold, turn out of the tin and carefully remove the paper.

Icing: Mix the icing sugar and hot water together until smooth. Pipe the icing in a lattice pattern over the cake and decorate with pieces of crystallised ginger.

Lemon Gingerbread (Vegan)

METRIC	IMP.	US.	
175g	6 oz	1 ½ cups	white self-raising flour
6 tbs.	6 tbs.	6 tbs.	vegetable margarine
3 tbs.	3 tbs.	3 tbs.	golden syrup
6 tbs.	6 tbs.	6 tbs.	brown sugar
2 tsp.	2 tsp.	2 tsp.	ground ginger
1 tsp.	1 tsp.	1 tsp.	mixed spice
2tbs.	2 tbs.	2 tbs.	crystallised ginger
2 tbs.	2 tbs.	2 tbs.	soya milk
125ml	8 tbs.	½ cup	water
			juice of 1 lemon

Preheat the oven to 180°C/350°F/Gas mark 4
Use a 900g/2 lb loaf tin.

Grease and line the loaf tin. Put the margarine, golden syrup and brown sugar into a pan and warm. Sieve all the dry ingredients into a bowl. Add the chopped ginger and stir in the syrup mixture. Add soya milk and stir until smooth. Bring the water and lemon juice to the boil and stir into the cake mixture. Pour the mixture into the prepared tin. Bake for 45-55 minutes. Cool in the tin.

Patterdale Pepper Cake

METRIC	IMP.	US.	
450g	1 lb	4 cups	white self-raising flour
2 tsp.	2 tsp.	2 tsp.	baking powder
1 tbs.	1 tbs.	1 tbs.	ground ginger
¼ tsp.	¼ tsp.	¼ tsp.	ground cloves
½ tsp.	½ tsp.	½ tsp.	freshly ground black pepper
100g	4 oz	½ cup	butter
225g	8 oz	1 cup	brown sugar
75g	3 oz	½ cup	seedless raisins
75g	3 oz	½ cup	currants
2 tbs.	2 tbs.	2 tbs.	cut mixed peel
175g	6 oz	½ cup	golden syrup, warmed
4 tbs.	4 tbs.	4 tbs.	sour cream
360ml	12 fl. oz	1½ cups	skimmed milk
			butter for greasing

Preheat the oven to 160°C/325°F/Gas mark 3
Use a deep 18cm/7 inch square cake tin.

Sift the flour, spices and black pepper into a mixing bowl. Rub in the butter until the mixture resembles fine breadcrumbs. Stir in the sugar and add the fruit and peel. Make a well in the flour mixture. Pour in the syrup, sour cream and milk and beat lightly.

Spoon the mixture into the prepared tin and bake for 2 ½ hours or until cooked through and firm to the touch. Cool on a wire rack.

Scandinavian Spice Cake

METRIC	IMP.	US.	
225g	8 oz	2 cups	white self-raising flour
4 tbs.	4 tbs.	4 tbs.	sour cream
100g	4 oz	½ cup	caster sugar
100g	4 oz	½ cup	butter, melted
1 tsp.	1 tsp.	1 tsp.	ground cloves
½ tsp.	½ tsp.	½ tsp.	ground ginger
½ tsp.	½ tsp.	½ tsp.	ground cardamom
125ml	8 tbs.	½ cup	buttermilk

Preheat the oven to 180°C/350°F/Gas mark 4
Use an 18cm/7 inch cake tin.

Grease the cake tin. Whisk the sour cream and sugar until light. Pour in the melted butter, sift in the dry ingredients and add the milk. Mix thoroughly. Turn the mixture into the prepared tin. Bake for about I hour or until a warm knife inserted into the centre comes out clean. Turn out on to a wire rack to cool.

Yoghurt and Molasses Cake

METRIC	***IMP.***	***US.***	
275g	10 oz	2 ½ cups	wholemeal self-raising flour
1 ½ tsp.	1 ½ tsp.	1 ½ tsp.	baking powder
300ml	½ pint	1 ¼ cups	plain yoghurt
275g	10 oz	1 cups	golden syrup
2 tbs.	2 tbs.	2 tbs.	molasses
2 tsp.	2 tsp.	2 tsp.	ground ginger
1 tsp.	1 tsp.	1 tsp.	cinnamon - ground
½ tsp.	½ tsp.	½ tsp.	ground cloves
6 tbs.	6 tbs.	6 tbs.	butter

Preheat the oven to 180°C/350°F/Gas mark 4
Use a 20cm/8 inch cake tin.

Grease and line the cake tin. Add the milk or yoghurt to the syrup and molasses. Sift the dry ingredients together and add them to the syrup mixture. Melt the butter and add to the mixture. Beat vigorously. Pour into the cake tin and bake for 45 minutes. Test with a warm knife inserted in to the centre of the cake. If it comes our clean, the cake is done. Leave to cool in the tin for ten minutes before turning out onto a wire rack.

Buttermilk Spice Cake

METRIC	IMP.	US.	
225g	8 oz	2 cups	white self-raising flour
½ tsp.	½ tsp.	½ tsp.	baking powder
½ tsp.	½ tsp.	½ tsp.	bicarb.
175g	6 oz	¾ cup	unsalted butter, softened
225g	8 oz	1 cup	soft brown sugar
2 tbs.	2 tbs.	2 tbs.	sour cream
1 tsp.	1 tsp.	1 tsp.	ground cinnamon
1 tsp.	1 tsp.	1 tsp.	ground cardamom
1 tsp.	1 tsp.	1 tsp.	ground cloves
75g	3 oz	½ cup	chopped raisins
250ml	8 fl. oz	1 cup	buttermilk

Preheat the oven to 180°C/350°F/Gas mark 4
Use a 23cm/9 inch square cake tin.

Grease and line the cake tin. Beat together the butter and the sugar until creamy. Add the sour cream and beat well. Sift the dry ingredients together, then sift again over the raisins and toss to mix through. Add alternate batches of the flour-raisin mixture and the buttermilk to the butter cream, about a third of each at a time. Fold in lightly but thoroughly. Do not overmix. Spoon the mixture into the cake tin, spreading evenly. Bake for an hour or until a warm knife inserted into the centre comes out clean.

Jewish Syrup Spice Cake

METRIC	IMP.	US.	
275g	10 oz	2 ½ cups	white self-raising flour
1 tsp.	1 tsp.	1 tsp.	bicarb. dissolved in 1 tbs. milk.
4 tbs.	4 tbs.	4 tbs.	butter
175g	6 oz	½ cup	golden syrup
4 tbs.	4 tbs.	4 tbs.	soft brown sugar
125ml	8 tbs.	½ cup	milk
6 tbs.	6 tbs.	6 tbs.	sour cream
1 tsp.	1 tsp.	1 tsp.	ground ginger
pinch.	pinch.	pinch.	of salt
1 tsp.	1 tsp.	1 tsp.	mixed spice
¼ tsp.	¼ tsp.	¼ tsp.	ground cloves
50g	2 oz	½ cup	flaked almonds

Preheat the oven to 180°C/350°F/Gas mark 4
Use a 20cm/8 inch round cake tin.

Grease and flour the cake tin. Place the butter, syrup and sugar in a small saucepan and place over a low heat, stirring constantly, until the sugar has dissolved. Remove from the heat and set aside.

Place the milk, sour cream and bicarb. mixture in a bowl and whisk. Sift the flour, ginger, salt, mixed spice and cloves into a large bowl. Make a well in the centre and pour in the syrup mixture and the milk and sour cream mixture. Use a metal spoon to mix the liquids together, gradually drawing in the flour. When all the flour has been incorporated and the mixture is smooth, pour the batter into the prepared cake tin. Sprinkle the flaked almonds evenly over the surface and press down very gently into the surface of the cake. Bake for about 1 hour or until the cake is cooked. Remove from the oven and leave in the tin for 30 minutes. Turn out on to a wire rack and leave until completely cold before serving.

Lincoln Buttermilk Cake

METRIC	*IMP.*	*US.*	
450g	1 lb	4 cups	white self-raising flour
2 tsp.	2 tsp.	2 tsp.	baking powder
225g	8 oz	1 cup	butter
1 tsp.	1 tsp.	1 tsp.	mixed spice (optional)
225g	8 oz	1 cup	sugar
1 tbs.	1 tbs.	1 tbs.	syrup
250g	9 oz	1 ½ cups	currants
1 tsp.	1 tsp.	1 tsp.	bicarb.
75g	3 oz	½ cup	dried mixed peel
600ml	1 pint	2 cups	buttermilk to mix (approx)

Preheat the oven to 180°C/350°F/Gas mark 4
Use a 900g/2 lb loaf tin.

Grease and line the loaf tin. Rub the butter into the flour and add the other dry ingredients. Warm the syrup and pour into the centre. Mix to a fairly soft mixture with the buttermilk. Bake in either two bread tins or in a deep slab cake tin for about one hour. Test with a warm knife. Allow to cool in the tin for fifteen minutes before turning out on a wire rack.

Coffee Fudge Cake

FOR THE CAKE

METRIC	IMP.	US.	
225g	8 oz	2 cups	white self-raising flour
½ tsp.	½ tsp.	½ tsp.	baking powder
175g	6 oz	¾ cup	soft butter
175g	6 oz	¾ cup	soft brown sugar
6 tbs.	6 tbs.	6 tbs.	sour cream
1 tbs.	1 tbs.	1 tbs.	decaffeinated instant coffee
125ml	8 tbs.	½ cup	milk

FILLING AND ICING

METRIC	IMP.	US.	
6 tbs.	6 tbs.	6 tbs.	soft butter
225g	8 oz	2 cups	icing sugar, sieved
1 tbs.	1 tbs.	1 tbs.	milk
1 tbs.	1 tbs.	1 tbs.	decaffeinated coffee
			a few shelled walnuts.

Preheat the oven to 180°C/350°F/Gas mark 4
Use two 20cm/8 inch sandwich tins.

Grease and line the sandwich tins. Measure all the ingredients for the cake into a bowl and beat well until thoroughly blended. Divide the mixture between the two tins and level out evenly. Bake in the oven for about 30 minutes until well risen and shrinking away slightly from the sides of the tins. Allow to cool for a few minutes, then turn out, peel off paper and finish cooling on a wire rack.

Filing and Icing: Measure all the ingredients into a bowl and beat well until thoroughly blended. Use half the mixture to sandwich the two cakes together, then stand on a serving plate and spread the remaining mixture on top. Mark decoratively with a fork and arrange some shelled walnuts on top.

Ginger and Walnut Teabread

METRIC	IMP.	US.	
225g	8 oz	2 cups	white self-raising flour
½ tsp.	½ tsp.	½ tsp.	baking powder
1 tsp.	1 tsp.	1 tsp.	salt
2 tsp.	2 tsp.	2 tsp.	ground ginger
4 tbs.	4 tbs.	4 tbs.	butter
4 tbs.	4 tbs.	4 tbs.	brown sugar
75g	3 oz	¾ cup	chopped walnuts
2tbs.	2 tbs.	2 tbs.	finely chopped crystallised ginger
2 tbs.	2 tbs.	2 tbs.	sour cream
125ml	8 tbs.	½ cup	milk
1 tsp.	1 tsp.	1 tsp.	demerara sugar

Preheat the oven to 180°C/350°F/Gas mark 4
Use a 450g/1 lb loaf tin.

Grease the loaf tin. Sift together the flour, salt, ginger and baking powder. Rub in the butter until the mixture resembles fine breadcrumbs. Mix in the sugar, walnuts and crystallised ginger. Mix most of the sour cream with the milk and add to flour and butter. Beat thoroughly. This makes a very sticky dough. Turn into the loaf tin. Brush the top with remaining sour cream and sprinkle with demerara sugar. Bake for 1 hour 5 minutes, until the teabread is golden brown and sounds hollow when tapped underneath. Serve sliced and buttered.

Cinnamon Bread

METRIC	IMP.	US.	
225g	8 oz	2 cups	white self-raising flour
½ tsp.	½ tsp.	½ tsp.	baking powder
1 tbs.	1 tbs.	1 tbs.	cinnamon
6 tbs.	6 tbs.	6 tbs.	butter
100g	4 oz	½ cup	brown sugar
4 tbs.	4 tbs.	4 tbs.	sour cream
½ tsp.	½ tsp.	½ tsp.	salt
250ml	8 fl. oz	1 cup	buttermilk
2 tsp.	2 tsp.	2 tsp.	vanilla
			extra 3 tbs. brown sugar

Preheat the oven to 180°C/350°F/Gas mark 4
Use a 450g/1 lb loaf tin.

Grease and line the tin. Sift the flour, salt, cinnamon and baking powder. Rub in the butter until the mixture resembles fine breadcrumbs. Mix in the sugar, vanilla, sour cream and the buttermilk. Pour into the tin and bake for 45 minutes. Leave to firm up for ten minutes before turning out onto a wire rack.

Fig, Walnut and Ginger Cake

METRIC	IMP.	US.	
225g	8 oz	2 cups	white self-raising flour
½ tsp.	½ tsp.	½ tsp.	baking powder
100g	4 oz	½ cup	butter
100g	4 oz	½ cup	caster sugar
75g	3 oz	½ cup	finely chopped figs
100g	4 oz	½ cup	finely chopped glacé ginger
50g	2 oz	½ cup	finely chopped walnuts
125ml	8 tbs.	½ cup	sour cream

Preheat the oven to 160°C/325°F/Gas mark 3
Use a 900g/2 lb loaf tin.

Grease the loaf tin and line the base with greaseproof paper. Grease the paper. Cream the butter and sugar in a small bowl until light and fluffy. Transfer the mixture to large bowl. Stir in figs, ginger and walnuts, then sifted flours and the sour cream. Spread the mixture into the prepared tin. Bake for about 1 ¼ hours. Stand 5 minutes before turning on to wire rack to cool.

Somerset Treacle Cake

METRIC	IMP.	US.	
225g	8 oz	2 cups	white self-raising flour
½ tsp.	½ tsp.	½ tsp.	baking powder
1 tsp.	1 tsp.	1 tsp.	mixed spice
100g	4 oz	½ cup	soft butter
6 tbs.	6 tbs.	6 tbs.	caster sugar
5 tbs.	5 tbs.	5 tbs.	black treacle
125ml	8 tbs.	½ cup	sour cream
75g	3 oz	½ cup	sultanas
			sieved icing sugar, for topping

Preheat the oven to 160°C/325°F/Gas mark 3
Use an 18cm/7 inch square cake tin.

Grease and line the cake tin with greased greaseproof. Using the all-in-one method, measure the flour, spice, soft butter, caster sugar, black treacle, sour cream and sultanas into one bowl and mix until all the ingredients are well blended. Turn the mixture into the prepared tin and level out the top. Bake in the oven for about 1 - 1 ¼ hours until a warm knife comes out clean when pushed into the centre of the cake. Turn on to a cooling tray. To serve, dust the top with sieved icing sugar.

Shearing Cake

METRIC	IMP.	US.	
400g	14 oz	3 ½ cups	white self-raising flour
1 tsp.	1 tsp.	1 tsp.	baking powder
pinch.	pinch.	pinch.	salt
225g	8 oz	1 cup	butter
225g	8 oz	1 cup	soft light brown sugar
1 tbs.	1 tbs.	1 tbs.	caraway seeds
1 tsp.	1 tsp.	1 tsp.	grated nutmeg or to taste
125ml	4 fl. oz	½ cup	sour cream
250ml	8 fl. oz	1 cup	milk
			grated rind of ½ lemon
			butter for greasing

Preheat the oven to 180°C/350°F/Gas mark 4
Use a 20cm/8 inch round cake tin.

Grease and line the cake tin. Sift the flour, salt and baking powder into a mixing bowl. Rub in the butter until the mixture resembles breadcrumbs, then stir in the sugar, lemon rind and spices. In a second bowl, mix the sour cream lightly with the milk, then stir gradually into the dry ingredients.

Spoon the mixture into the prepared tin and bake for 1 ½ hours or until cooked through and firm to the touch, covering the surface with a piece of greased paper or foil if it browns too quickly. Cool for 10 minutes in the tin, then invert on a wire rack to cool completely.

Seed Cake

FOR THE CAKE

METRIC	IMP.	US.	
225g	8 oz	2 cups	white self-raising flour
½ tsp.	½ tsp.	½ tsp.	baking powder
2 tsp.	2 tsp.	2 tsp.	caraway seeds
100g	4 oz	½ cup	butter
100g	4 oz	½ cup	caster sugar
1 tbs.	1 tbs.	1 tbs.	double cream
125ml	8 tbs.	½ cup	milk (approx)

TOPPING:

METRIC	IMP.	US.	
1 tbs.	1 tbs.	1 tbs.	caster sugar
1 tsp.	1 tsp.	1 tsp.	caraway seeds

Preheat the oven to 180°C/350°F/Gas mark 4
Use a 20cm/8 inch deep round cake tin.

Grease and line the cake. Sift the flour baking powder and salt. Rub in butter until the mixture resembles fine breadcrumbs. Add seeds and mix in lightly with a fork. Add cream and milk. The mixture should be of a sticky consistency. Top with castor sugar and caraway seeds mixed together. Pour into prepared tin and bake for 1 hour. Cool on a wire rack. Serve while the cake is hot.

Greek Orange Spice Cake.

METRIC	IMP.	US	
275g	10 oz	2 ½ cups	wholemeal self-raising flour
1 tsp.	1 tsp.	1 tsp.	bicarb.
½ tsp.	½ tsp.	½ tsp.	ground cloves
½ tsp.	½ tsp.	½ tsp.	cinnamon
175g	6 oz	¾ cup	brown sugar
175g	6 oz	¾ cup	butter
250ml	8 fl. oz	1 cup	orange juice
50g	2 oz	¼ cup	chopped walnuts
75g	3 oz	½ cup	raisins
			a few sesame seeds

Preheat the oven to 180°C/350°F/Gas mark 4
Use a 900g/2 lb loaf tin.

Grease and line the cake tin. Sift together the flour, baking powder and spices in a large bowl. Rub in the butter. Mix in the walnuts and raisins. Gradually pour in the orange juice. Mix well.

Spoon into the prepared tin, and sprinkle with sesame seeds. Bake for 40-50 minutes in the preheated oven. Test with a warm knife. When done, remove from the oven and allow to cool in the tin for 20 minutes. Turn out onto a wire rack to cool completely.

Coffee & Walnut Ring

FOR THE CAKE

METRIC	IMP.	US.	
225g	8 oz	2 cups	white self raising flour
100g	4 oz	½ cup	dark muscovado sugar
4 tbs.	4 tbs.	4 tbs.	sour cream
3 tbs.	3 tbs.	3 tbs.	instant coffee - decaff.
175g	6 oz	¾ cup	butter
50g	2 oz	½ cup	shelled walnuts, chopped
125ml	8 tbs.	½ cup	warm milk

ICING AND DECORATION

METRIC	IMP.	US.	
1 tsp.	1 tsp.	1 tsp.	instant coffee - decaff.
1 tbs.	1 tbs.	1 tbs.	hot water
50g	2 oz	½ cup	icing sugar, sifted
8	8	8	walnut halves

Preheat the oven to 180°C/350°F/Gas mark 4
Use a 1.25 litre/2 pint ring mould.

Lightly grease the ring mould. Cream the butter with the sugar until light and fluffy. Gradually beat in the sour cream. Mix the coffee powder and warm milk and beat into the mixture. Fold in the flour and chopped walnuts, then stir in the milk. Spoon into the prepared mould and smooth the surface.

Bake in the preheated oven for 45 - 50 minutes until well risen and firm to the touch. Cool slightly before carefully turning out of the mould onto a wire rack.

Glacé icing: Mix the coffee powder with the hot water. Add to the icing sugar, mixing in well. Carefully pour over the ring, allowing some icing to trickle over the sides. Decorate with the walnut halves.

Raspberry Spice Cake.

FOR THE CAKE

METRIC	IMP.	US.	
175g	6 oz	1 ½ cups	white self-raising flour
6 tbs.	6 tbs.	6 tbs.	butter
6 tbs.	6 tbs.	6 tbs.	caster sugar, firmly packed
2 tsp.	2 tsp.	2 tsp.	cinnamon
½ tsp.	½ tsp.	½ tsp.	allspice
1 tsp.	1 tsp.	1 tsp.	nutmeg
7 tbs.	7 tbs.	7 tbs.	sour cream
250g	9 oz	¾ cup	raspberry jam, sieved
50g	2 oz	½ cup	finely chopped walnuts

GLAZE

METRIC	IMP.	US.	
150g	5 oz	½ cup	raspberry jam
125ml	8 tbs.	½ cup	apple juice
2 tsp.	2 tsp.	2 tsp.	arrowroot
3 drops.	3 drops.	3 drops.	lemon juice

Preheat the oven to 180°C/350°F/Gas mark 4
Use two 23cm/9 inch sandwich tins.

Grease the tins. Cream the butter and sugar in a bowl until light. Add the sour cream and beat. Sift the flour and spices together. Fold the dry ingredients into the mixture and blend. Fold in the jam and walnuts, then pour into the tins and bake for 25-30 minutes. Leave in the tins for five minutes, then turn out on a wire rack to cool.

Glaze: Combine jam and apple juice in a pan. Bring to the boil and simmer for 5-6 minutes, then remove from heat. Mix arrowroot with 1 tbs. water and stir in. Return to the heat and bring to the boil. Stir in lemon juice and set aside. When cold, carefully split each cake in half. Spread the glaze on three of the cake layers, sandwich all together and spread the top and sides with the remaining glaze

Syrup and Spice Teabread

The easiest way to measure large quantities of syrup or treacle is to weigh the tin or jar, without the lid, then from this weight deduct the amount needed in the recipe. Spoon out from the container until the scales register the calculated amount.

METRIC	IMP.	US.	
275g	10 oz	2 ½ cups	white self-raising flour
½ tsp.	½ tsp.	½ tsp.	bicarb.
½ tsp.	½ tsp.	½ tsp.	baking powder
pinch.	pinch.	pinch.	of salt
1 tsp.	1 tsp.	1 tsp.	ground mixed spice
1 tsp.	1 tsp.	1 tsp.	ground ginger
1 tsp.	1 tsp.	1 tsp.	ground cinnamon
4 tbs.	4 tbs.	4 tbs.	butter
175g	6 oz	½ cup	golden syrup
175g	6 oz	¾ cup	demerara sugar
75g	3 oz	½ cup	finely chopped mixed peel
2 tbs.	2 tbs.	2 tbs.	sour cream
125ml	8 tbs.	½ cup	milk
			flaked almonds, to decorate

Preheat the oven to 180°C/350°F/Gas mark 4
Use a 900g/2 lb loaf tin.

Grease and line the loaf tin with greaseproof paper. Melt the butter in a small saucepan. Remove from the heat and stir in the syrup and sugar. Leave to cool. Sift the flour, salt, raising agents and spices into a bowl and mix in the chopped peel. Mix the sour cream and milk together and mix thoroughly with the cooled syrup mixture. Pour into the dry ingredients and beat until smooth. Pour the mixture into the prepared tin and scatter flaked almonds over it. Bake in the oven for 1 ¼ hours or until well risen and firm to the touch. Turn out and cool on a wire rack.

Fochabers Gingerbread

METRIC	IMP.	US.	
450g	1 lb	4 cups	white self-raising flour
1 tsp.	1 tsp.	1 tsp.	bicarb.
1 tsp.	1 tsp.	1 tsp.	baking powder
225g	8 oz	1 cup	butter
100g	4 oz	½ cup	brown sugar
225g	8 oz	¾ cup	black treacle
4 tbs.	4 tbs.	4 tbs.	sour cream
1 tsp.	1 tsp.	1 tsp.	ground ginger
1tbs.	1 tbs.	1 tbs.	mixed spice
pinch.	pinch.	pinch.	of ground cloves
pinch.	pinch.	pinch.	of ground cinnamon
75g	3 oz	½ cup	currants
75g	3 oz	½ cup	sultanas
75g	3 oz	½ cup	chopped candied peel
75g	3 oz	¾ cup	ground almonds
300ml	½ pint	1 ¼ cups	apple juice

Preheat the oven to 160°C/325°F/Gas mark 3
Use a 23cm/9 inch cake tin.

Grease and line the cake tin. Cream the butter and sugar. Add the slightly warmed treacle. Add the sour cream and beat the mixture. Mix the flour and baking powder with the spices, dried fruit and almonds. Dissolve the bicarb. in the apple juice and gradually mix all the ingredients together. Spoon into the prepared tin and bake for two hours. Test with a warm knife. Leave to firm up in the tin for fifteen minutes before turning out on a wire rack to cool completely.

Guernsey Buttermilk Cake

METRIC	IMP.	US.	
450g	1 lb	4 cups	white self-raising flour
1 tsp.	1 tsp.	1 tsp.	bicarb.
1 tsp.	1 tsp.	1 tsp.	baking powder
250g	9 oz	1 ½ cups	currants
125ml	8 tbs.	½ cup	apple juice
100g	4 oz	½ cup	unsalted butter
1 tsp.	1 tsp.	1 tsp.	grated nutmeg
225g	8 oz	1 cup	brown sugar
4 tbs.	4 tbs.	4 tbs.	sour cream
125ml	8 tbs.	½ cup	buttermilk
2 tsp.	2 tsp.	2 tsp.	lemon juice

Preheat the oven to 160°C/325°F/Gas mark 3
Use a 20cm/8 inch cake tin.

Grease and line the cake tin. Steep the currants in the apple juice until plumped. Rub the butter into the flour until the mixture resembles fine bread crumbs. Sift together the nutmeg, baking powder, bicarb. and sugar and add to the mixture. Mix the sour cream into the buttermilk with the lemon juice. Make a well in the dry ingredients. Mix in the apple juice, with the steeped currants and the buttermilk alternately, adding about one-third each time. Mix thoroughly to blend. Place the mixture in the cake tin and bake for two hours or until the cake is springy and brown. Cool well before cutting.

Cumberland Buttermilk Cake

METRIC	IMP.	US.	
450g	1 lb	4 cups	white self-raising flour
1 tsp.	1 tsp.	1 tsp.	baking powder
1 tsp.	1 tsp.	1 tsp.	bicarb.
175g	6 oz	¾ cup	butter
100g	4 oz	½ cup	brown sugar
175g	6 oz	1 cup	chopped candied lemon peel
75g	3 oz	½ cup	seedless raisins
2 tbs.	2 tbs.	2 tbs.	marmalade
250ml	8 fl. oz	1 cup	buttermilk

Preheat the oven to 160°C/325°F/Gas mark 3
Use a 20cm/8 inch cake tin.

Grease and line the cake tin. Sift the flour and baking powder and rub in the butter until the mixture resembles fine bread crumbs. Add the sugar. Scatter the peel and raisins over the surface. Mix the marmalade into the milk, warming to dissolve. Allow to cool. Mix the soda into the milk mixture, and use it to mix the dry ingredients to a soft dough. Place in the cake tin and bake for one hour. Lower the heat to 150C/300F/gas mark 2, and bake for a further forty five minutes or until the cake is springy and browned. Cool well before cutting.

Poppy Seed Cake

METRIC	IMP.	US.	
225g	8 oz	2 cups	wholemeal self-raising flour
1 tsp.	1 tsp.	1 tsp.	baking powder
75g	3 oz	½ cup	poppy seeds
250ml	8 fl. oz	1 cup	skimmed milk
100g	4 oz	½ cup	butter, softened
100g	4 oz	½ cup	light soft brown sugar
6 tbs.	6 tbs.	6 tbs.	sour cream

Preheat the oven to 180°C/350°F/Gas mark 4
Use a 20cm/8 inch round cake tin.

Grease and base line the cake tin. Put the poppy seeds into a pan with the milk and bring to the boil. Set aside to cool completely. In a large mixing bowl, beat the butter and sugar together until pale and fluffy. Add the sour cream. Sift the flour into a bowl, adding any residue of bran left in the sieve. Fold the flour into the creamed mixture, then stir in the poppy seeds and milk. Spoon the mixture into the tin and level the surface.

Bake for about 1 hour, or until the cake has risen and browned and is beginning to shrink from the sides of the tin. Leave to firm up in the tin for 5 - 10 minutes, then turn out onto a wire tray. Peel off the lining paper and allow to cool.

German Spice Cake

FOR THE CAKE

METRIC	IMP.	US.	
450g	1 lb	4 cups	wholemeal self-raising flour
2 tsp.	2 tsp.	2 tsp.	baking powder
275g	10 oz	1 cup	golden syrup
½ tsp.	½ tsp.	½ tsp.	powdered cardamon
pinch.	pinch.	pinch.	cloves
pinch.	pinch.	pinch.	salt
225g	8 oz	1 cup	sugar
6 tbs.	6 tbs.	6 tbs.	butter
125ml	8 tbs.	½ cup	sour cream
75g	3 oz	½ cup	currants
50g	2 oz	½ cup	nibbed or chopped almonds
250ml	8 fl. oz	1 cup	orange juice
75g	3 oz	½ cup	candied lemon peel
75g	3 oz	½ cup	candied orange peel
½ tsp.	½ tsp.	½ tsp.	lemon rind
½ tsp.	½ tsp.	½ tsp.	orange rind

FILLING

METRIC	IMP.	US.	
250g	9 oz	¾ cup	apricot jam
			marzipan

CAROB ICING

METRIC	IMP.	US.	
225g	8 oz	2 cups	icing sugar
2 tbs.	2 tbs.	2 tbs.	carob powder
1 tsp.	1 tsp.	1 tsp.	butter
5 tbs.	5 tbs.	5 tbs.	hot water

Preheat the oven to 180°C/350°F/Gas mark 4
Use 2 Swiss Roll Trays

Grease the Swiss Roll trays. Heat gently together the syrup, sugar and butter until the sugar has dissolved and the butter melted. Take off the heat and stir in the spices. Set aside to cool.

Sift the flour with the salt and baking powder twice, then into a bowl. Stir in the melted ingredients, and add the lemon and orange rind and sour cream. Combine well. Add the candied peels, fruits, and nuts, and finally the orange juice. Pour the mixture into the two prepared trays. They should be about half full, as the mixture rises well in baking. Bake in the preheated oven for 35 - 40 minutes. Remove and allow to cool in the trays for ten minutes, before turning out onto a wire rack.

Filling: Split each cake in half when cool. Spread a quarter of the apricot jam over the bottom layer and cover with a layer of cake. Roll the marzipan on a sheet of greaseproof paper dredged with icing sugar until it is large enough to fit the cake. Brush the cake first with more apricot jam, then sandwich the marzipan with it. Cover with another layer of cake which has first been coated with apricot jam, and brush the top of this with the jam too. Cover with the last piece of cake. Ice the whole of the cake with carob icing and decorate with a few split almonds.

Carob Icing: Sift icing sugar and carob powder into a bowl, stir in the combined butter and water. Beat until smooth.

Coffee Almond Slice

FOR THE CAKE

METRIC	IMP.	US.	
175g	6 oz	1 ½ cups	white self raising flour
100g	4 oz	½ cup	butter
100g	4 oz	½ cup	sugar
8 tbs.	8 tbs.	8 tbs.	sour cream
50g	2 oz	½ cup	ground almonds
2	2	2	drops almond essence
125ml	8 tbs.	½ cup	water

FILLING AND DECORATION

METRIC	IMP.	US.	
2 tbs.	2 tbs.	2 tbs.	carob chips
300ml	½ pint	1 ¼ cups	double cream
2tbs.	2 tbs.	2 tbs.	instant decaffeinated coffee
1 tbs.	1 tbs.	1 tbs.	hot water
50g	2 oz	½ cup	icing sugar

Preheat the oven to 180°C/350°F/Gas mark 4
Use an 18 x 28cm/7 x 11 in deep cake tin.

Grease and line the cake tin. Put all the ingredients in a bowl. Mix together and beat until smooth. Pour the batter into the prepared tin. Bake for 25 to 30 minutes until firm to the touch. Turn out, remove paper and cool.

Filling and decoration: Melt the carob chips until runny and keep warm. Whisk the cream with the dissolved coffee and icing sugar until it forms soft peaks. Trim the edges of the cake and cut into three even-sized pieces. Spread a layer of cream on one piece, top with a second layer and spread with more cream. Top with the final layer of cake. Spread the sides with cream. Spoon the carob into a piping bag with a fine nozzle. Pipe straight lines along the length of the cake and draw lines backwards and forwards across the carob lines creating a chevron effect. Chill for at least one hour and serve.

Coffee and Pecan Cake.

FOR THE CAKE

METRIC	IMP.	US.	
225g	8 oz	2 cups	white self-raising flour
1 tsp.	1 tsp.	1 tsp.	baking powder
1 tbs.	1 tbs.	1 tbs.	cinnamon
pinch.	pinch.	pinch.	ginger
1 tsp.	1 tsp.	1 tsp.	nutmeg
2 tsp.	2 tsp.	2 tsp.	allspice
1 tsp.	1 tsp.	1 tsp.	salt
100g	4 oz	½ cup	butter
100g	4 oz	½ cup	brown sugar
250m1	8 fl oz	1 cup	sour cream
100g	4 oz	1 cup	pecan nuts, chopped

FILING AND ICING

METRIC	IMP.	US.	
225g	8 oz	2 cups	icing sugar
6 tbs.	6 tbs.	6 tbs.	carob powder
1 tbs.	1 tbs.	1 tbs.	instant decaffeinated coffee
175g	6 oz	¾ cup	butter
4 tbs.	4 tbs.	4 tbs.	boiling water
			a few extra pecan nuts

Preheat the oven to 160°C/325°F/Gas mark 3
Use two 23cm/9 inch springform tins.

Grease the tins. Sift the dry ingredients. Whisk the butter and sugar until light. Mix in the sour cream. Beat in the nuts and the dry ingredients, taking care not to overbeat. Divide the mixture between the two tins and bake in the pre-heated oven for 40 minutes. When the cake starts to shrink away from the rides, remove from the oven and turn out on a wire rack.

Filling and icing: Combine the sifted icing sugar and carob in bowl with butter. Stir in the combined coffee and water. Fill the cake, cover the top and coat the sides. Decorate with a few pecan nuts.

FOOD FOR LIFE.

CAKES MADE WITH VEGETABLES.

The problems of homelessness and starvation are not confined to countries in the third world. In Britain, there are tens of thousands sleeping rough on city streets, many begging during the day to buy food. Srila Prabhupada wanted to set up a feeding programme whereby no-one within ten miles of a Hare Krishna temple would go hungry. Food for Life is the result.

Food for Life is the only vegetarian feeding programme. In fact food is offered to Krishna, so that those who receive it also get spiritual benefit. Presently, in Britain, Food for Life operates in ten cities. A free food cafe has been established in Manchester, catering to the low-waged and students.

There is a great demand for Food for Life in Eastern Europe, where countries are going through economic upheaval and civil war. Devotees in Sarajevo receive food shipments which they prepare for locals in this war torn city. Devotees in Sukhumi, Georgia also cater to the victims of civil strife. Polish devotees run a large Food for Life programme and Moscow members try to satisfy the demand in that country.

Food for Life also operates in India and Africa. The Durban temple in South Africa has a team which goes out each day to the black African townships. In Vrndavana, northern India, plans are underway to build a prasadam hall, where widows and others who have retired to this holy place can get a nutritious prasadam meal. A similar project in Mayapur, West Bengal has operated for twenty years.

Please make a contribution to Food for Life. We are limited only by the resources we have. There is a great deal of enthusiasm among our members to make this programme successful. Your donation will make a real difference. Please send your cheque to:

ISKCON Food for Life, 2 St James Road, Watford, WD1 8EA, UK.

Thank you. Bhagavat.

Sour Cream Carrot Cake

FOR THE CAKE

METRIC	IMP.	US.	
175g	6 oz	1 ½ cups	white self-raising flour
1 tsp.	1 tsp.	1 tsp.	ground cinnamon
1 tsp.	1 tsp.	1 tsp.	ground nutmeg
100g	4 oz	½ cup	brown sugar
225g	8 oz	2 cups	grated carrot
125ml	8 tbs.	½ cup	vegetable oil
125ml	8 tbs.	½ cup	sour cream

CREAM CHEESE ICING

METRIC	IMP.	US.	
100g	4 oz	½ cup	packaged cream cheese softened
4 tbs.	4 tbs.	4 tbs.	soft butter
1 tsp.	1 tsp.	1 tsp.	grated lemon rind
225g	8 oz	2 cups	icing sugar

Preheat the oven to 160°C/325°F/Gas mark 3
Use a 20cm/8 inch ring tin.

Grease the ring tin. Line the base with greaseproof paper. Grease the paper. Sift together the flour, cinnamon and nutmeg in bowl. Stir in the sugar and grated carrot. Combine the oil and sour cream. Stir into the flour mixture. Pour the mixture into the prepared tin. Bake in for about 50 minutes. Turn on to wire rack to cool. When cold, spread with icing. Decorate with walnut halves.

Icing: Beat the cream cheese, butter and lemon rind in small bowl until light and fluffy. Gradually beat in the sifted icing sugar. Beat until combined.

Carrot and Orange Cake.

FOR THE CAKE

METRIC	IMP.	US.	
175g	6 oz	¾ cup	butter
1 tbs.	1 tbs.	1 tbs.	grated orange rind
175g	6 oz	¾ cup	caster sugar
8 tbs.	8 tbs.	8 tbs.	sour cream
250g	9 oz	1 ½ cups	sultanas
150g	5 oz	1 ¼ cups	coarsely grated carrot
225g	8 oz	2 cups	white self-raising white flour
1 tsp.	1 tsp.	1 tsp.	ground nutmeg
1 tsp.	1 tsp.	1 tsp.	mixed spice
8 tbs.	8 tbs.	8 tbs.	orange juice

ORANGE ICING

METRIC	IMP.	US.	
6 tbs.	6 tbs.	6 tbs.	butter
150g	5 oz	1 ¼ cup	icing sugar
1 tbs.	1 tbs.	1 tbs.	orange juice
			few drops orange food colouring

Preheat the oven to 160°C/325°F/Gas mark 3
Use a 900g/2 lb loaf tin.

Grease the loaf tin. Line the base with greaseproof paper. Grease the paper. Cream the butter, rind and sugar in small bowl until light and fluffy. Add the sour cream and mix until well combined. Transfer the mixture to large bowl, stir in sultanas and grated carrot, then the sifted dry ingredients and orange juice. Spread into the prepared tin. Bake for 1 ½ hours. Stand for five minutes before turning on to wire rack to cool. Top with icing when cake is cold.

Orange Icing: Beat butter in small bowl until light and fluffy, gradually beat In sifted icing sugar, then juice and a little colouring; beat until smooth.

Carrot, Raisin and Walnut Loaf (Vegan)

METRIC	IMP.	US.	
175g	6 oz	1 ½ cups	white self-raising flour
175g	6 oz	¾ cup	vegetable margarine.
1 tsp.	1 tsp.	1 tsp.	vanilla essence
175g	6 oz	¾ cup	brown sugar
2 tbs.	2 tbs.	2 tbs.	golden syrup
125ml	8 tbs.	½ cup	soya milk
175g	6 oz	1 ½ cups	grated carrot
175g	6 oz	1 cup	chopped raisins
100g	4 oz	1 cup	chopped walnuts
½ tsp.	½ tsp.	½ tsp.	ground nutmeg
½ tsp.	½ tsp.	½ tsp.	ground cinnamon

Preheat the oven to 180°C/350°F/Gas mark 4
Use a 1.4kg/3 lb loaf tin.

Grease and line the loaf tin. Cream the margarine, essence and sugar in small bowl until light and fluffy. Beat in the golden syrup, then the soya milk. Beat until combined. Transfer the mixture to large bowl. Stir in the carrot, raisins and walnuts. Stir in the sifted dry ingredients. Stir until combined. Pour the mixture into the prepared tin. Bake for about 1 ¼ hours. Stand for five minutes before turning on to wire rack to cool.

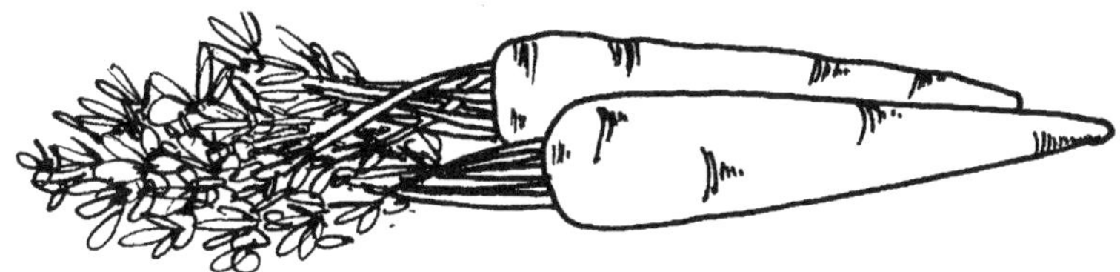

Swiss Carrot Cake

FOR THE CAKE

METRIC	IMP.	US.	
225g	8 oz	2 cups	white self-raising flour
½ tsp.	½ tsp.	½ tsp.	baking powder
175g	6 oz	¾ cup	light muscovado sugar
50g	2 oz	½ cup	walnuts, chopped
100g	4 oz	1 cup	grated carrots
2	2	2	large ripe bananas, mashed
4 tbs.	4 tbs.	4 tbs.	sour cream
125ml	8 tbs.	½ cup	sunflower oil

TOPPING

METRIC	IMP.	US.	
6 tbs.	6 tbs.	6 tbs.	soft butter
100g	4 oz	½ cup	cream cheese
175g	6 oz	1 ½ cups	icing sugar, sieved
4 tbs.	4 tbs.	4 tbs.	plain yoghurt

Preheat the oven to 180°C/350°F/Gas mark 4
Use a 20cm/8 inch round cake tin.

Grease and line the cake tin. Measure the flour and baking powder into a large bowl and stir in the sugar. Add the nuts, carrot and banana, and mix lightly. Make a well in the centre and add the sour cream and oil. Beat well until blended. Turn into the tin and bake in the oven for about 1 ¼ hours until the cake is golden brown, and is shrinking slightly from the sides of the tin. A warm knife pushed into the centre should come out clean. Turn out, remove the paper, and leave to cool on a wire rack.

Topping: Measure all the ingredients together in a bowl and beat well until blended and smooth. Spread over the cake and rough up with a fork. Leave in a cool place to harden slightly before serving. Serve cut into thin wedges.

Carrot Coffee Cake.

FOR THE CAKE

METRIC	IMP.	US.	
275g	10 oz	2 ½ cups	white self-raising flour
1 tsp.	1 tsp.	1 tsp.	baking powder
100g	4 oz	½ cup	butter
175g	6 oz	¾ cup	brown sugar
2 tbs.	2 tbs.	2 tbs.	sour cream
½ tsp.	½ tsp.	½ tsp.	mixed spice
1 tbs.	1 tbs.	1 tbs.	grated orange rind
2 tbs.	2 tbs.	2 tbs.	orange juice
125ml	8 tbs.	½ cup	strong black coffee - decaff.
150g	5 oz	1 ¼ cups	carrots, grated
75g	3 oz	¾ cup	chopped walnuts

TOPPING.

METRIC	IMP.	US.	
100g	4 oz	½ cup	soft cream cheese
4 tbs.	4 tbs.	4 tbs.	unsalted butter
100g	4 oz	1 cup	icing sugar
1 tsp.	1 tsp.	1 tsp.	vanilla essence
			juice of ½ lemon.

Preheat the oven to 180°C/350°F/Gas mark 4
Use a 20cm/8 inch round cake tin.

Grease and line the tin. Cream the butter and the sugar until light. Whisk in the sour cream, mixed spice, orange rind, juice and coffee. Toss the carrots and walnuts in the flour and gradually stir into the mixture. Pour the mixture into the tin and bake for 1 ½ hours. Cool in the tin for half an hour. Remove and finish cooling on a wire rack.

Topping: Cream the cheese and butter together. Slowly sift in the icing sugar and continue beating until the mixture is quite smooth. Stir in the vanilla and lemon juice. Spread 2/3 of the mixture on top of the carrot cake. Place the remainder in a piping bag and pipe rosettes around the cake.

Carrot and Walnut Cake

METRIC	IMP.	US.	
200g	7 oz	1 ¾ cups	white self-raising flour
½ tsp.	½ tsp.	½ tsp.	baking powder
225g	8 oz	1 cup	brown sugar
175g	6 oz	¾ cup	butter
175g	6 oz	1 ½ cups	grated carrots
½ tsp.	½ tsp.	½ tsp.	salt
1 tsp.	1 tsp.	1 tsp.	cinnamon
½ tsp.	½ tsp.	½ tsp.	grated nutmeg
2 tbs.	2 tbs.	2 tbs.	sour cream
75g	3 oz	½ cup	raisins
50g	2 oz	½ cup	chopped walnuts
125ml	8 tbs.	½ cup	milk

Preheat the oven to 180°C/350°F/Gas mark 4
Use a 20cm/8 inch round cake tin.

Grease and line the cake tin. Place the butter in a saucepan and melt over a very low heat. Pour the melted butter into a large mixing bowl and add sugar, carrot, salt, cinnamon, nutmeg and sour cream. Sift the flour and baking powder into the bowl and add raisins and walnuts, fold in thoroughly with the milk. Spoon the mixture into the prepared tin and bake for about an hour until firm to touch. Cool in tin for 10 minutes then transfer to wire rack to cool completely.

Vegan Pumpkin Fruitcake

METRIC	IMP.	US	
175g	6 oz	1 ½ cups	wholewheat flour
1 tsp.	1 tsp.	1 tsp.	bicarb.
1 tsp.	1 tsp.	1 tsp.	baking powder
100g	4 oz	½ cup	brown sugar
1 tsp.	1 tsp.	1 tsp.	ground cinnamon
½ tsp.	½ tsp.	½ tsp.	ground nutmeg
¼ tsp.	¼ tsp.	¼ tsp.	ground allspice
¼ tsp.	¼ tsp.	¼ tsp.	ground gloves
50g	2 oz	½ cup	walnuts, chopped
75g	3 oz	½ cup	raisins
175g	6 oz	1 cup	dried figs, chopped
175g	6 oz	1 cup	pumpkin, fresh cooked
6 tbs.	6 tbs.	6 tbs.	vegetable oil
125ml	4 fl. oz	½ cup	fresh orange juice
			grated rind of orange

Preheat the oven to 160°C/325°F/Gas mark 3
Use a 900g/2 lb loaf tin.

Combine the juice, raisins and figs in a bowl. Leave to stand for at least 1 hour, preferably overnight.

Grease and line the loaf tin. Mash together the pumpkin, sugar and oil. Stir in the soaked fruit mixture and mix well. Add the flour, baking soda, baking powder and spices. Mix well. Stir in the walnuts and orange rind. Spoon the batter into the prepared loaf tin. Bake in the preheated oven for 40 to 45 minutes, or until a warm knife inserted in the centre comes out clean. Leave to cool in the tin for 15 minutes. Turn out and cool on a wire rack.

Carrot Cake

METRIC	IMP.	US.	
225g	8 oz	2 cups	white self-raising flour
½ tsp.	½ tsp.	½ tsp.	baking powder
100g	4 oz	½ cup	butter
100g	4 oz	½ cup	brown sugar
2 tsp.	2 tsp.	2 tsp.	finely grated orange rind
3 tbs.	3 tbs.	3 tbs.	grated carrot
2 tbs.	2 tbs.	2 tbs.	sour cream
125ml	8 tbs.	½ cup	milk

Preheat the oven to 180°C/350°F/Gas mark 4
Use an 18cm/7 inch cake tin.

Grease and flour the cake tin. Sift the flour and baking powder. Rub in butter until the mixture resembles fine breadcrumbs. Add sugar, orange rind and grated carrot. Mix thoroughly, then add sour cream orange juice and milk. Spoon into the prepared tin and bake for 1 hour and 10 minutes. Cool on wire rack.

Easy-Mix Carrot Cake

METRIC	IMP.	US.	
175g	6 oz	1 ½ cups	wholemeal self-raising flour
½ tsp.	½ tsp.	½ tsp.	bicarb.
125ml	8 tbs.	½ cup	sour cream
½ tsp.	½ tsp.	½ tsp.	ground cinnamon
2	2	2	medium carrots, grated
225g	8 oz	1 cup	butter, melted
175g	6 oz	¾ cup	brown sugar, firmly packed
250g	9 oz	1 ½ cups	sultanas

Preheat the oven to 180°C/350°F/Gas mark 4
Use a 900g/2 lb loaf tin.

Grease the loaf tin. Line the base and sides with greaseproof paper. Grease the paper well. Combine the sour cream, bicarb. cinnamon and carrots until well blended. Add the butter and sugar. Mix well. Stir in the sifted flour and sultanas. Pour into the prepared tin. Bake for about 50 minutes. Stand for five minutes before turning on to wire rack to cool.

Carrot and Prune Cake

METRIC	IMP.	US.	
175g	6 oz	1 ½ cups	white self-raising flour
1 tbs.	1 tbs.	1 tbs.	mixed spice
175g	6 oz	1 cup	pitted prunes
75g	3 oz	½ cup	sultanas
75g	3 oz	¾ cup	pecan nuts
175g	6 oz	¾ cup	soft brown sugar
5 tbs.	5 tbs.	5 tbs.	oil
175g	6 oz	1 ½ cups	grated carrots
6 tbs.	6 tbs.	6 tbs.	yoghurt
125ml	8 tbs.	½ cup	sour cream

Preheat the oven to 160°C/325°F/Gas mark 3
Use a 20cm/8 inch cake tin.

Grease and line the cake tin. Coarsely chop the pecans and prunes. Sift the and mixed spice together. Stir in pecans, sultanas and prunes. Mix sour cream, yoghurt and sugar together until well blended. Add to the dry ingredients and beat until evenly distributed. Pour the mixture into the prepared tin and bake for 1 and ¼ hours. Stand for at least ten minutes before turning out to cool on a wire rack.

Pumpkin Cake.

METRIC	IMP.	US.	
225g	8 oz	2 cups	white self-raising flour
½ tsp.	½ tsp.	½ tsp.	baking powder
225g	8 oz	1 cup	butter
225g	8 oz	1 cup	caster sugar
4 tbs.	4 tbs.	4 tbs.	sour cream
1 tbs.	1 tbs.	1 tbs.	finely grated orange rind
½ tsp.	½ tsp.	½ tsp.	almond essence
250g	9 oz	1 ½ cups	chopped dates
50g	2 oz	½ cup	ground almonds
225g	8 oz	1 ½ cups	mashed, cooked pumpkin
100g	4 oz	½ cup	finely chopped crystallised ginger
pinch.	pinch.	pinch.	of salt
125ml	8 tbs.	½ cup	milk

Preheat the oven to 180°C/350°F/Gas mark 4
Use a deep 20cm/8 inch square cake tin.

Grease and line the cake tin. Cream the butter with sugar in a bowl until light and fluffy. Add the sour cream and beat well. Stir in the orange rind, almond essence, chopped dates, ground almonds, mashed pumpkin and ginger until combined. Sift the flour, baking powder and salt together and fold into the mixture, alternately, with the milk until blended.

Place the mixture into the prepared cake tin and smooth the surface, Bake for 50 - 60 minutes. Test with a warm knife. Cool in the tin for ten minutes before turning out on a wire rack.

Potato Ginger Cake

FOR THE CAKE

METRIC	IMP.	US.	
150g	5 oz	1 ¼ cups	white self-raising flour
100g	4 oz	½ cup	butter
6 tbs.	6 tbs.	6 tbs.	brown sugar
4 tbs.	4 tbs.	4 tbs.	sour cream
175g	6 oz	½ cup	golden syrup
2 tsp.	2 tsp.	2 tsp.	ground ginger
1 tsp.	1 tsp.	1 tsp.	ground cinnamon
75g	3 oz	½ cup	grated raw potato

LEMON ICING

METRIC	IMP.	US.	
225g	8 oz	2 cups	icing sugar
1 tsp.	1 tsp.	1 tsp.	butter
1 tbs.	1 tbs.	1 tbs.	lemon juice, approximately

Preheat the oven to 180°C/350°F/Gas mark 4
Use a 900g/2 lb loaf tin.

Grease and line the loaf tin. Cream the butter and sugar in a small bowl until light and fluffy. Add the sour cream and mix well. Gradually beat in the golden syrup. Transfer the mixture to a large bowl. Stir in the sifted dry ingredients and potato. Pour into the prepared tin and bake for about 1 ¼ hours. Stand for ten minutes before turning on to wire rack to cool. Spread the cold cake with icing.

Lemon Icing: Sift the icing sugar into a small heat proof bowl. Stir in the butter and enough lemon juice to make a stiff paste. Stir over hot water until the icing is spreadable.

Potato Carob Cake

FOR THE CAKE

METRIC	IMP.	US.	
150g	5 oz	1 ¼ cups	white self-raising flour
175g	6 oz	¾ cup	butter
175g	6 oz	¾ cup	caster sugar
4 tbs.	4 tbs.	4 tbs.	sour cream
150g	5 oz	1 ¼ cups	cold mashed potato
75g	3 oz	½ cup	carob chips
125ml	8 tbs.	½ cup	milk

CAROB ICING

METRIC	IMP.	US.	
100g	4 oz	½ cup	butter
225g	8 oz	2 cups	icing sugar
2 tbs.	2 tbs.	2 tbs.	carob powder
2 tbs.	2 tbs.	2 tbs.	milk, approximately

Preheat the oven to 180°C/350°F/Gas mark 4
Use a 20cm/8 inch ring tin.

Grease and line the ring tin. Cream the butter and sugar in a small bowl until light and fluffy. Add the sour cream and mix well. Stir in the potato with half the sifted flour and carob and half the milk. Stir in the remaining flour, carob and milk. Spread the mixture into the prepared tin. Bake for about 40 minutes. Stand ten minutes before turning on to wire rack to cool. Spread the cold cake with icing.

Carob Icing: Beat the butter in a small bowl until creamy. Gradually beat in sifted icing sugar and carob and milk, beat until icing is spreadable.

Tomato Raisin Loaf

METRIC	IMP.	US.	
175g	6 oz	1 ½ cups	white self-raising flour
50g	2 oz	½ cup	wholemeal self-raising flour
½ tsp.	½ tsp.	½ tsp.	baking powder
175g	6 oz	¾ cup	butter, softened
175g	6 oz	¾ cup	caster sugar
1 tsp.	1 tsp.	1 tsp.	grated lemon rind
4 tbs.	4 tbs.	4 tbs.	sour cream
200g	7 oz	1 cup	peeled chopped tomatoes
75g	3 oz	½ cup	chopped raisins
25g	1 oz	¼ cup	chopped nuts
1 tsp.	1 tsp.	1 tsp.	mixed spices
¼ tsp.	¼ tsp.	¼ tsp.	salt

Preheat the oven to 180°C/350°F/Gas mark 4
Use a 900g/2 lb loaf tin.

Grease and line the loaf tin. Cream together the butter, sugar and lemon rind. Add the sour cream. Beat well. Press the tomatoes through a sieve to remove the seeds. Add the pulp to the butter-cream and add the raisins and nuts. Sift the dry ingredients over the butter-tomato mixture and fold through. Spoon into the loaf tin. Bake for 35 to 40 minutes. Remove from the oven and allow to stand for ten minutes before carefully turning out onto a cake rack to cool.

Courgette Cake (Vegan)

Small, young courgettes can be shredded with their skins intact. Older vegetables should be peeled and have their seeds removed first.

METRIC	IMP.	US.	
175g	6 oz	1 ½ cups	white self-raising flour
4 tbs.	4 tbs.	4 tbs.	soya milk
100g	4 oz	½ cup	brown sugar
75g	3 oz	¼ cup	golden syrup
125ml	8 tbs.	½ cup	corn oil
1 tsp.	1 tsp.	1 tsp.	mixed spices
¼ tsp.	¼ tsp.	¼ tsp.	salt
75g	3 oz	½ cup	sultanas
25g	1 oz	¼ cup	chopped walnuts
100g	4 oz	1 cup	grated courgette

Preheat the oven to 180°C/350°F/Gas mark 4
Use a 900g/2 lb loaf tin.

Grease and line the cake tin. Place the soya milk in a small bowl. Add the sugar, golden syrup and corn oil and beat well until smooth. Sift the flour, spices and salt into a large bowl and make a well in the centre. Add the soya milk-sugar mixture and stir through lightly with a wooden spoon. Add the sultanas, walnuts and grated courgette and fold through to combine thoroughly. Turn into the cake tin. Bake for 55 to 60 minutes. Remove from the oven and allow to stand for ten minutes before carefully turning out onto a cake rack to cool.

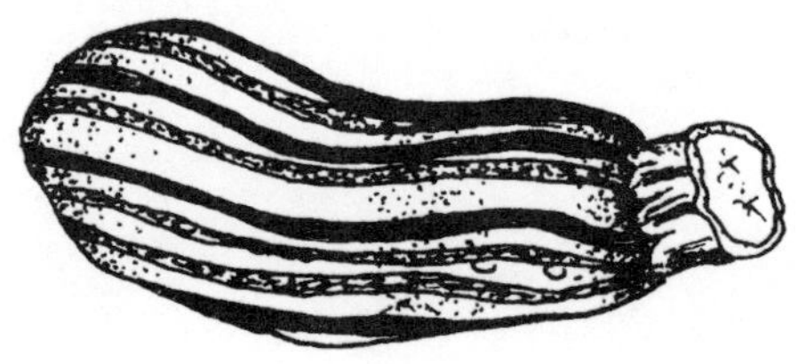

American Potato Cake

METRIC	IMP.	US.	
150g	5 oz	1 ¼ cups	white self-raising flour
½ tsp.	½ tsp.	½ tsp.	baking powder
50g	2 oz	½ cup	carob powder
½ tsp.	½ tsp.	½ tsp.	cinnamon
½ tsp.	½ tsp.	½ tsp.	nutmeg
½ tsp.	½ tsp.	½ tsp.	cloves
175g	6 oz	¾ cup	caster sugar
1 tbs.	1 tbs.	1 tbs.	vanilla sugar
225g	8 oz	1 cup	butter
8 tbs.	8 tbs.	8 tbs.	sour cream
8 tbs.	8 tbs.	8 tbs.	milk
75g	3 oz	½ cup	raisins
50g	2 oz	½ cup	chopped almonds
100g	4 oz	1 cup	warm, mashed potato
			rind of ½ lemon

Preheat the oven to 180°C/350°F/Gas mark 4
Use a 23cm/9 inch square cake tin.

Grease and line the cake tin. Dust the raisins and nuts with a little flour. Sift half the remaining flour with the spices and carob and the other half with the baking powder. Set aside.

Cream the sugars and the butter until light and fluffy. Beat in the mashed potato and the sour cream. Mix in the spiced flour and blend well. Then stir in the milk and add the rest of the flour. Stir in the nuts, raisins and lemon rind. Pour the cake batter into the prepared tin and bake in the preheated oven for one hour, or until a warm knife inserted into the centre comes out clean. Leave to cool in the tin for ten minutes, then turn out to cool on a wire rack.

Tomato and Spice Cake

FOR THE CAKE

METRIC	IMP.	US.	
450g	1 lb	4 cups	white self-raising flour
1 tsp.	1 tsp.	1 tsp.	baking powder
1 tsp.	1 tsp.	1 tsp.	bicarb.
175g	6 oz	¾ cup	butter
225g	8 oz	1 cup	brown sugar
2 tsp.	2 tsp.	2 tsp.	vanilla essence
1 tsp.	1 tsp.	1 tsp.	cinnamon
1 tsp.	1 tsp.	1 tsp.	nutmeg
½ tsp.	½ tsp.	½ tsp.	ground cloves
½ tsp.	½ tsp.	½ tsp.	mixed spice
575g	1 ¼ lb	1 ¾ lb	fresh tomatoes, pureed
75g	3 oz	½ cup	chopped pecans

ICING

METRIC	IMP.	US.	
100g	4 oz	½ cup	cream cheese
4 tbs.	4 tbs.	4 tbs.	butter
150g	5 oz	1 ¼ cup	icing sugar
1 tsp.	1 tsp.	1 tsp.	cinnamon
1 tsp.	1 tsp.	1 tsp.	nutmeg, for garnish

Preheat the oven to 180°C/350°F/Gas mark 4
Use a 23cm/9 inch ring tin.

Grease and line the tin. Beat the butter with the sugar and vanilla until light and creamy. Fold in the sifted flour, baking powder, bicarb. and spices. Stir in the tomato puree and pecans. Pour the batter into the tin and bake for 60 - 70 minutes, or until a warm knife inserted in the centre comes out clean. Cool in the tin for ten minutes, then turn onto a wire rack. Ice when cold.

Icing: Beat the cream cheese and butter until smooth. Gradually beat in the icing sugar and cinnamon. Top the cake with icing and sprinkle with nutmeg.

Beetroot and Carob Cake

METRIC	*IMP.*	*US*	
225g	8 oz	2 cups	white self-raising flour
1 tsp.	1 tsp.	1 tsp.	baking soda
¾ cup	¾ cup	¾ cup	carob powder
1 tbs.	1 tbs.	1 tbs.	cornstarch
50g	2 oz	¼ cup	brown sugar
½ tsp	½ tsp	½ tsp	salt
75g	3 oz	½ cup	raisins
1	1	1	medium beetroot, cooked and chopped
1 tsp.	1 tsp.	1 tsp.	vanilla essence
¾ cup	¾ cup	¾ cup	boiling water
125ml	4 fl. oz	½ cup	boiling water

Preheat the oven to 180°C/350°F/Gas mark 4
Use a 23cm/9 inch square cake tin.

Grease and line the cake tin. Put the raisins in a small bowl and pour over ½ cup boiling water. Set aside to steep for 30 minutes. In a large bowl, blend together the carob and ¾ cup boiling water. Set aside to cool.

Sift together the flour, soda, and salt in a large bowl. Puree the raisins and water with a hand mixer or blender. Add the beetroot and ¾ of a cup of cool water to the puree. Blend further. Dissolve the cornstarch in ¼ cup warm water. Stir the raisin and beetroot puree, the dissolved cornstarch, the sugar and vanilla into the carob mixture.

Stir the flour and dry ingredients into the carob mixture. Do not stir longer than needed to thoroughly mix the two. Spoon the batter into the prepared tin and smooth the surface. Bake on the top shelf for 35 to 40 minutes, or until a warm knife inserted in the middle of the cake comes out clean.

Cool in the tin for 10 to 15 minutes and then remove to a wire rack. Cool the cake completely before cutting.

Pumpkin Pecan Cake (Vegan)

FOR THE CAKE

METRIC	IMP.	US.	
225g	8 oz	2 cups	white self-raising flour
½ tsp.	½ tsp.	½ tsp.	baking powder
225g	8 oz	1 ½ cups	pumpkin
175g	6 oz	¾ cup	vegetable margarine
175g	6 oz	¾ cup	caster sugar
2 tbs.	2 tbs.	2 tbs.	golden syrup
4 tbs.	4 tbs.	4 tbs.	soya milk
100g	4 oz	1 cup	pecan nuts, chopped
1 tsp.	1 tsp.	1 tsp.	ground cinnamon

TOPPING:

METRIC	IMP.	US.	
2 tbs.	2 tbs.	2 tbs.	golden syrup
¼ tsp.	¼ tsp.	¼ tsp.	ground cinnamon
8-12	8-12	8-12	pecan nuts
2 tbs.	2 tbs.	2 tbs.	pumpkin seeds

Preheat the oven to 160°C/325°F/Gas mark 3
Use an 18cm/7 inch round cake tin.

Grease and line the tin. Peel the pumpkin, chop and boil in a little water for 2-3 minutes until tender. Drain and mash. Beat the margarine, sugar and syrup together in a bowl until light. Add the soya milk. Stir in the pumpkin and nuts. Sift the flour and cinnamon together over the mixture and carefully fold in. Place the mixture in the tin, smooth, and bake for 70 minutes, or until cake springs back when pressed. Cool for 10 mins. Turn out onto a wire rack.

Topping: Heat the syrup and cinnamon in a small pan. Bring to the boil, then remove from the heat. Brush the top of cake with the glaze and decorate with pecan nuts and pumpkin seeds. Brush the nuts and seeds with more glaze.

Carrot and Parsnip Loaf

METRIC	*IMP.*	*US.*	
225g	8 oz	2 cups	wholemeal self-raising flour
1 tsp.	1 tsp.	1 tsp.	baking powder
6 tbs.	6 tbs.	6 tbs.	sour cream
50g	2 oz	½ cup	porridge oats
75g	3 oz	½ cup	parsnips, scraped
175g	6 oz	¾ cup	light soft brown sugar
225g	8 oz	1 cup	skimmed milk cottage cheese
150g	5 oz	1 ¼ cups	fresh, hard carrots, scraped
1 tsp.	1 tsp.	1 tsp.	finely snipped fresh rosemary

Preheat the oven to 180°C/350°F/Gas mark 4
Use a 900g/2 lb loaf tin.

Grease and line the loaf tin. Reduce the cottage cheese to a finer texture by either passing it through a food processor for a few minutes or pressing it through a sieve. Put the smooth cheese into a large mixing bowl, add the sugar and beat well. Beat in the sour cream.

Grate the carrots and parsnips into small pieces and add them to the mixture. Sift the flour and baking powder into the mixture. Stir in the rolled oats and rosemary. Mix all the ingredients thoroughly. Spoon the mixture into the tin and level the surface. Bake for about 1 hour, or until the loaf is firm and starting to shrink from the sides of the tin. Leave in the tin for ten minutes, then turn out to cool on a wire tray.

Carrot Tea Bread

METRIC	IMP.	US.	
175g	6 oz	1 ½ cups	wholemeal self-raising flour
½ tsp.	½ tsp.	½ tsp.	baking powder
1 tsp.	1 tsp.	1 tsp.	ground cinnamon
pinch.	pinch.	pinch.	salt
100g	4 oz	1 cup	grated carrot
175g	6 oz	¾ cup	butter
175g	6 oz	¾ cup	light soft brown sugar
6 tbs.	6 tbs.	6 tbs.	sour cream
50g	2 oz	½ cup	walnuts, finely chopped
			a little milk
			grated rind of ½ large orange

Preheat the oven to 160°C/325°F/Gas mark 3
Use a 450g/1 lb loaf tin.

Grease and line the loaf tin. Sift the flour, cinnamon, salt and baking powder into a mixing bowl, adding any residue of bran left in the sieve. Stir in the grated carrot and mix well.

In a large mixing bowl, cream the butter and sugar until pale and fluffy. Beat in the orange rind. Mix the sour cream into the creamed mixture, a little at a time. Fold in the flour mixture together with the walnuts, adding a little milk to give a soft, but not runny, consistency.

Spoon the mixture into the tin and level the top. Bake for about one hour until the loaf is risen, firm to the touch and just beginning to shrink from the sides of the tin. Leave to firm up in the tin for ten minutes then turn out onto a wire tray.

APPENDIX

INGREDIENTS USED IN THIS BOOK.

All-bran

A breakfast cereal, rich in bran. Any compacted bran flake type cereal will do.

Candied or Glacé Fruit

Candied and Glacé fruits start off with the same process of successive boiling in more and more concentrated solutions of sugar and glucose. Glacé fruit, after drying, is dipped in crack-boiled sugar.

Candied Peels

The candied peel of various citrus fruits which has been boiled and soaked in sugar syrup. It can vary enormously in quality. Try to get peel which is not too hard.

Carob

A good, healthy substitute for Chocolate. See the Carob cakes chapter.

Coconut

Normally encountered as desiccated coconut - the flesh is ground and dried. Coconut cream is now widely available, and even coconut milk can be found in Indian shops. Using fresh ground Coconut flesh in a cake is a revelation.

Dried Fruit

Apricots

Most dried apricots are produced in California, Australia, South Africa, Turkey and Iran. Nowadays most of the fruits are treated with sulphur dioxide. Some health food shops sell Turkish unsulphured apricots. These are dark, sweet and very sticky.

Banana Chips

Banana chips contain less than five percent of their original moisture. Grinding them produces banana flour.

Currants, Raisins and Sultanas

Collectively known as vine fruits in the food trade, all are produced from various types of sun-dried grapes. Sultanas are unfamiliar in the US. They are a large variety of raisin. Buy vine fruits young, before they get a sugary crystalline coating.

Dates

Dried dates for baking should be soft and sticky, not hard and dry. Don't buy dull looking dates, or those with a white bloom.

Figs

Dried figs should be full and succulent. Reject figs which look thin, and have too much skin. Yellowish varieties often taste sweeter.

Mixed Fruit

Mixed fruit is a basic mixture of vine fruits, sometimes including tropical fruits such as papayas, pineapple and mango. Some mixtures can contain dried peel.

Prunes

Prunes are actually a variety of dried plums. Buy large prunes, which look dark and glossy.

Essences

Try to use natural essences. In Western countries at least, they are now freely available.

Almond Essence

This is a strong flavouring which must be used with care. Overuse adds a very synthetic flavour to a cake.

Peppermint Essence

Count the drops very carefully. The adventurous cook can try using the fresh leaves..

Vanilla Essence.

The synthetic version is very widely used, although it is possible to get the natural version.

Rosewater

A sweet dilute essence, prepared from Rose Petals. Common in Indian and Arabic sweets.

Fats and Oils.

Butter

There are three main types of Butter - Salted, Slightly Salted and Unsalted. The latter is the more expensive and harder to come by. It is popular in Continental European recipes. If you cannot find it, substitute either of the other two.

Corn Oil

Made from the pressed germ of Maize. Good for frying.

Sunflower Oil

This oil is widely used because of its high content of poly-unsaturated oils, which not only don't add to the level of blood cholesterol, but help to bring it down.

Vegetable Oil

Common oil, made from Rape Seed, the yellow fields of which are frequently seen in Southern England.

Vegetable Margarine

Used for Vegan recipes. Much less expensive than butter, this gives good results. Generally 80% fat. There are two types, hard and soft. Soft margarine is useful for making one-stage cakes.

Other Oils

Other oils that can be used in baking include Olive Oil (be careful, it has a strong flavour), Sesame Oil, Safflower Oil (high in poly-unsaturates), edible Coconut Oil, Peanut Oil, Poppy Seed oil and Soya Oil.

Flours and Grains

Corn Flour

Produced from maize, corn flour is practically pure starch. It contains no gluten. Corn flour is a very good thickening agent. It rarely forms lumps.

Wheat Flours

There are many types of wheat. For our purposes, there is strong wheat, which has a flinty, translucent grain, and soft wheat, which is opaque and soft. This latter type of wheat is the best for cakes, the former is suited better for breadmaking.

Plain Flour (All Purpose Flour)

Soft flour, known as plain flour in England is called all-purpose flour in the US. Cake flour is also sold as such in the US

Self-Raising Flour

Self-raising flour is a made by adding a raising agent to a soft cake flour. It is widely available in Britain, Australia, New Zealand and South Africa, but it is rare in Europe and the US. Readers in these countries should follow the following recipe;

To make your own self-raising flour, sift together the following ingredients

1 cup/4 oz/100gm soft, all purpose, plain flour.
1 teaspoon baking powder
1/8 teaspoon bicarbonate of soda.

Wholemeal Flour

Wheat flour from which some or all of the bran has not been removed. More dense than ordinary flours, wholemeal flour may not rise as much. Also available as a self-raising variety in some countries.

Potato Flour

Often used in the Scandinavian countries as a thickener. Instant potato mix can be used as a substitute where it is not available.

Soya Flour

Soya is the success product of the 20th century, at least in the West. It was known and used long before in China and Japan. The flour ground from the beans is full of protein.

Fresh Fruit

Apples

Avoid apples which are too young and tart, or too old and powdery. For Apple Puree add a little lemon juice to prevent it from turning brown.

Apricots

Make sure the fruit is fully ripe, the flesh should be orange. For apricot nectar, liquidise 1 cup of ripe apricots with ½ cup of water.

Banana

The best fruit for cakes is that which is fully ripe, with the skin just developing brown spots. Speed up the ripening, if necessary, by storing in a brown paper bag at room temperature.

Blueberries

Common in the US, but rare in Europe, where Bilberries make a good substitute.

Gooseberries

Use them ripe, at the height of their flavour.

Lemons

Lemons are grown commercially on a large scale in the Mediterranean countries, and in California and Arizona. The Lemon tree will only flourish in frost free regions. Lemons are generally picked and shipped before they are ripe. They are also generally treated with chemicals and wax. It is possible to get unwaxed organically grown Lemons in some areas. To experience the full flavour, you must pick one off the tree yourself.

Limes

There are two basic types of lime:
1)The South Asian or Indian type, which is small, yellow and has a thin skin.
2) The Tahiti lime, which is green, larger and has a thick skin.
Both types are suitable for cake-making.

Oranges

Reject fruit on which the skin is bruised, and bear in mind that loose skin Oranges are more perishable than the tight skinned varieties.

Passion Fruit.

Also known as Grenadilla and Maracuga. Choose fruits that are still firm and round, before the skin becomes crinkly. They should be deep purple in colour. Guavadillas are a good substitute. They have a light green to beige colouring.

Pears.

Use unblemished fruit for the best results.

Pineapples.

Only buy a Pineapple in a supermarket if it has a sweet, pleasant smell. reject fruit if the skin is soft, or if the smell is pungent. Pineapples must be ripe when you buy them, they will not ripen up in a warm place at home.

Plums.

There are many varieties of plums, most of which are interchangeable. They should be bought close to the time of use, as they go off rapidly.

Fruit Juices

Apple Juice

Some recipes we adapted called for alcoholic drinks. We have generally substituted apple juice, or apple juice concentrate. The concentrate can in many cases substitute portions of the sugar in a recipe, (see Sugar Substitutes). They will add an extra dimension to the flavour of the cake.

Lemon, Lime and Orange juice.

Freshly made juice is best. All three are available in cartons or bottles. The bought product often contains sulphur dioxide which some people are allergic to.

Grape Juice.

In some cases, we substituted grape juice in a recipe where wine or wine derivatives were called for. The concentrated juice can be used in place of sugar. (see Sugars and Sweeteners)

Passion Fruit Juice.

Passion Fruits, also known as Grenadilla or Maracuga, are becoming widely available. They are generally expensive, and it may be more economical to use commercial Passion Fruit Juice.

Pineapple Juice.

Fresh juice is of course the best, but many of us live far from the nearest Pineapple plantation. Look out on the supermarket shelves for juice that has not been re-constituted from a concentrate.

Jams and Preserves

Apricot Jam

Plum Jam

Raspberry Jam

Pear and Apple spread

Fresh Jams are best with home-made cakes. They can be made with less sugar than normal jam. Pear and Apple spread is a good sugar substitute, available in wholefood shops.

Milk Products

Buttermilk.

In may cases, yoghurt diluted with a little water can be used in place of buttermilk, although strictly speaking cultured buttermilk is produced from milk by a different culture.

Cream

Double Cream

Known as Heavy Cream in the US. Double Cream has a minimum butterfat content of 48%. It can be diluted with milk to extend it.

Whipping Cream

Whipping Cream has a minimum butterfat content of 35%. This is a medium cream, used for whipping

Single Cream

Known in the US as Light Cream, or half-and-half. This is a pouring cream with 18% butterfat.

Sour Cream

This is single cream which has a bacterium added for souring. The culture forms an acid which gives a flavour and helps thickening. it keeps well under refrigeration. Used throughout the book as a substitute for eggs. Sour Cream can be made in the home by adding a tablespoon of Lemon Juice to a cup of single or double cream.

Cheese

Cream Cheese

Soft cheese with a high cream content, sometimes called Philadelphia Cheese. Curd Cheese, with less fat content can also be used.

Cottage Cheese

Soft cheese with large curds. Commonly made with skimmed milk.

Hard Cheese

Vegetarian hard cheeses are becoming more popular. Cheddar goes particularly well with Apple and Walnuts.

Milk

Milk nowadays is full of things that Scientists have put into it. If you can get a good source that a Scientist has not yet had a chance to get at, you are a lucky person. The worst things that Scientists put in milk are the growth hormones used to fatten up the cows. These can bring on early puberty in human children. Other things to avoid include fish oil, compulsory in the US.

Evaporated Milk

Milk boiled under reduced pressure. generally unsweetened. Good with fruit.

Condensed Milk

Available sweetened (Nestlés) or unsweetened. Recipes in the book use the former, a thick syrupy product, much loved by children if they can get there hands on it.

Milk Powder

Skimmed milk powder is common, but the full cream variety is a little harder to find. Check out Asian and Indian grocers.

Skimmed or Semi-Skimmed Milk

Milk with all the fat taken out, suitable for people with a low-calorie diet.

Yoghurt

Generally available yoghurt is made from skimmed milk, with skimmed milk powder added. Bio-yoghurt with a German culture is popular now in Europe. It is thick and creamy. Avoid stiff low-fat yoghurt, it often contains gelatine. The best yoghurt - you guessed it - is made at home.

Nuts

Nuts are used for flavour, texture and decoration. Check that nuts are fresh when you buy them. Don't buy in large quantities, as they have a tendency to lose their taste and go rancid.

Almonds.

Almonds are perhaps the worlds most popular nut. They are grown in Mediterranean countries and in California. There are two types of Almonds, sweet and bitter. Bitter almonds are rare, and should not be eaten in quantity, as they contain a cyanide derivative. Almonds can be bought whole, split, blanched, flaked and ground.

Hazelnuts.

Hazelnuts are also known as cob-nuts, Kent cobs and filberts (particularly in the US). The tree from which they are derived belongs to the birch family. There are usually used ground in cakes. Before using for decoration, the thin inner covering of the Hazelnut should be removed. Heat the nuts in the oven or under a low grill. Then tip the hot nuts onto a clean tea-towel and rub until the papery skins slip off..

Peanuts.

Strictly speaking, Peanuts are legumes. They are originate in South America. Pound for pound, they have more protein than meat, more calories than sugar and more oil than cream. They are the cheapest nuts to buy. They are widely used in making biscuits. Peanut butter is a tasty ingredient for icings and filling.

Pecan Nuts.

Pecans are a native of North America. They are also known as Hickory nuts. They are interchangeable with Walnuts in any recipe. They are claimed to have the highest fat content of any vegetable food, with a calorie count close to that of butter.

Pine Kernels.

Also known as Pine Nuts. Gathered from various pine trees. Popular in the Middle-East. Have a subtle resinous flavour. If you find these hard to track down, try an Arab grocer.

Pistachios.

Grown from Afghanistan to Mediterranean, and also in the United States. They are invaluable for decoration.

Walnuts.

Popular since classical Greek and Roman times. The lighter the Walnuts, the better flavour. If you want nuts to chop, it is often economical to buy them already halved. Be careful not to burn Walnuts, they become very bitter.

Mixed Nuts

Take care when buying Mixed Nuts. Check that they are not bulked out with Peanuts.

Raising agents

Self-raising flour is a curious ingredient. Widely available in Britain, Australia, New Zealand and South Africa it is rare in Europe and the US. Readers in these countries should pay special attention to the information below. A recipe for Self-raising flour is given under 'Flours and Grains' in this section.

Bicarbonate of Soda.

At one time, all rising was done with yeast, which reacts with sugar, producing tiny bubbles of carbon dioxide gas in a dough. Bicarbonate of soda produces the same effect, but only in the presence of an acid, such as lemon juice, cream of tartar or sour milk.

Baking Powder.

Baking powder contains bicarbonate as well as an acid (usually an acid phosphate), in solid form. It begins to work when you mix a liquid with the dough, and works a second time when heated in the oven.

Cream of Tartar (Tartaric Acid)

Cream of Tartar is made from powdered dried grapes. It can be added to a recipe along with Bicarbonate of Soda to produce the raising gas.

Salt

Salt is used in very small quantities in cakes. Most salt in the supermarket is chemically produced, although there is now a trend to use sea salt and other natural salts.

Seeds

Caraway seeds

Common in Austrian and German recipes. The seed should be bought whole and crushed as needed..

Poppy seeds

Popular in Poland and Germany, and in traditional Jewish recipes. Blue-grey seeds are common in the West, pale cream seeds are common in the East.

Pumpkin Seeds

Dry roast the seeds for a few moments before use to bring out the flavour.

Sesame seeds

Dry roast or fry in a little oil before use until they give off a roasted aroma or until they just change colour.

Soya Milk

Made from the Soya Bean, a staple food in China and Japan. A good substitute for milk and milk products for those who have decided to follow a Vegan diet.

Spices

Allspice

Combines the flavour of cloves, cinnamon and nutmeg, although it is not a related species. Very popular in Scandinavian recipes. Occurs as small berries. Try to buy in berry form and grind when needed. The ground spice does not store well.

Cardamon

The Cardamon plant is related to Ginger. Black Cardamon is not used in baking. The seeds of the pale green and white cardamons are ground and used in cakes and breads. Popular in Scandinavia and Germany.

Cinnamon

Bark of the Cinnamon tree. There are two main types, Cinnamon and Cassia. The latter has a stronger flavour. Cassia is generally used for curries and Indian cooking. Cinnamon's delicate flavour is more suitable for baking. Cinnamon can be bought as sticks or quills and ground in a coffee grinder before use, although buying the freshly ground spice is more convenient.

Cloves

Cloves are the flower buds of a tropical evergreen tree. They should be used very sparingly.

Ginger

The ground dried root of the Ginger plant. Like all spices, it is good for digestion. Adventurous cooks may try to use fresh ginger in baking. you must use a small quantity, it has a more powerful taste.

Mace

Mace is the dried *aril* or cage occurring around the nutmeg. It has a subtly different flavour..

Mixed Spice

Bought in the shop, mixed spice can be stale. Make your own by mixing one part ground cloves, two parts ginger, four parts cinnamon and four parts nutmeg.

Mustard Powder

Rare in baking, sometimes used in gingerbread.

Rosemary

Rare in baking. Not strictly a spice, but a herb used in other branches of cooking.

Sugars and Sweeteners.

It is generally acknowledged that Westerners eat too much white refined sugar. As this is matter of personal choice, we have generally used the same sugar in our recipes as the originals from which they were adapted. There are, however, a number of healthier alternatives on the market.

Black Treacle

An early product of the sugar-refining process. Black treacle is sweeter and more subtle than Molasses. High in Iron.

Brown Sugar

Dark Brown Sugar, Light Brown Sugar. Most commercial brown sugar is white sugar with a little molasses added.

Caster Sugar

Known in the US as Superfine Sugar or Bakers Special Sugar. This is ground to a smaller particle size to help it dissolve more easily, and give an even texture. In countries where this is not available, grind granulated sugar in a coffee grinder.

Cube Sugar

This is produced by moulding and pressing granulated sugar with sugar syrup.

Demarara Sugar

This is a refined sugar produced from a partly discoloured syrup. It contains about two percent of natural molasses. It can replace white sugar in any recipe.

Granulated Sugar

Generally the cheapest, widely available type of sugar. All minerals and extra nutrients are filtered out before this sugar is crystallised.

Golden Syrup

A syrup made from refined sugar plus invert sugar, plus a little sugar colouring. Unavailable in the US, where Corn Syrup should be substituted.

Honey

Generally we have avoided using Honey where it is cooked. Indian tradition informs us that cooking Honey can bring out toxins.

Icing Sugar

Known as Confectioners or Powdered sugar in the US. Also sometimes known as 10X sugar. This is made by grinding sugar crystals to a fine powder. Generally cornflour is added to prevent caking. It is not used for basic cake mixtures, as it produces a poor volume and hard crust. generally used only for icing and decorating.

Malt Extract

A thick sticky brown syrup produced from germinated Barley grains. Consists mainly of maltose. Use Corn Syrup or Treacle if you cannot get it.

Maple Syrup

Maple Syrup is produced by tapping the sap of the North American Maple tree. It contains a high proportion of sugar and has a distinctive flavour.

Muscovado Sugar

Also known as Barbados Sugar. Extracted after the mother liquor has made three trips through the centrifuge. It is the last time the producer can extract sugar from the almost exhausted source. The crystals are small and coated with molasses.

Molasses

Molasses is the rich concentrated syrup remaining after almost all the sucrose has been extracted from the sugar liquor. It contains some sucrose, and other types of sugars along with all the vitamins and minerals missing from white sugar. High in Iron, Copper, Calcium, magnesium, Phosphorus, Chromium, Potassium and Zinc. The darker the molasses, the less sugar it contains. Try to find unsulphured molasses, its lighter and better flavoured.

Sugar Substitution.

There are many types of sugar which we have not used in this book, but which you may have a preference for. It may be that a particular kind of sugar is unavailable in your part of the world. Below are some suggestions for substitutes to the common granulated sugar, volume for volume.

Alternative Sweetener	Substitute this amount for each cup of sugar	Reduce total liquid by this amount for each cup.
Maple Syrup	¾ US cup (190 ml)	2 Tablespoons
Maple Sugar Granules	1 US cup (150g / 5 oz)	
Rice Syrup	1 ¼ US cups (310 ml)	6 Tablespoons
Honey	¾ US cup (190 ml)	2 Tablespoons
Date Sugar	1 US cup (150g / 5 oz)	
Malt Extract	1 ¼ US cups (310 ml)	6 Tablespoons
Conc. Fruit Juice	1 ½ US cups (360 ml)	1 ½ US cups (360 ml)
Molasses	½ US cup (120 ml)	
Gur or Jaggery	1 US Cup (150g / 5 oz)	

Based on an original table in Lord Krishna's Cuisine, by Yamuna Devi, published by Bala/Angus and Robertson, 1987.

Tea and Coffee

Decaffeinated Coffee

A healthy alternative flavouring. Coffee, like chocolate, is full of caffeine and other unhealthy alkaloids. You can also use Barleycup and other grain coffees in perhaps slightly greater quantities.

Peppermint and Rosehip Tea

Herbs and herb teas have great potential as flavourings in baking. One which we haven't mentioned is Lemon Balm. Experiment!

Thickening Agents

Arrowroot.

Arrowroot can be used in sauces and glazes. It thickens at a lower temperature than cornflour, and does not have to be cooked to remove it's raw taste.

Cornflour.

Known as Cornstarch in the US. Used for sauces and glazes. Can also be incorporated into a cake to give good flavour.

Vegetables

Before sugar was common, cakes were made with sweet vegetables. Some of the recipes are with us today.

Carrots

Young sweet carrots, which are free from discoloration are best for cakes.

Courgette (Zucchini)

Either use young vegetables, or remove the skin of older specimens.

Parsnips

Avoid roots which are discoloured. The later in the year the Parsnip is picked, the sweeter the root.

Potatoes

New potatoes give the most flavour to Potato cakes. Older potatoes are milder, and may be more suitable, according to your taste.

Pumpkin

There is a large variety of pumpkins, and they can generally be used interchangeably in cakes. Butternuts are a personal favourite.

Tomatoes

Tomatoes are treated as a fruit in the US, and a vegetable in Europe. Choose fresh tomatoes for cakes, avoid those with tough skin. Before use, cut out and discard the stem and its root.

INDEX

A

Abbreviations ... xvi
Africa. ... 111
All-bran ... 193
Allspice ... 200
Allspice Malt Ring ... 140
Almond and Apricot Cake (Vegan) ... 113
Almond Cake ... 118
Almond Essence ... 194
Almonds. ... 198
American Fudge Cake. ... 26
American Potato Cake ... 187
Appendix ... 193
Apple and Cinnamon Cake ... 64
Apple and Walnut Teabread ... 80
Apple Buttermilk Cake ... 70
Apple Juice ... 196
Apple Molasses Cake (Vegan) ... 73
Apple Sauce Cake (Vegan) ... 66
Apple Spice Loaf ... 62
Apple, Cheese and Nut Loaf ... 65
Apples ... 195
Apricot Bran Bread ... 96
Apricot Cake. ... 92
Apricot Carob Chip Cake ... 19
Apricot Fruit Loaf ... 107
Apricot Jam ... 197
Apricot Upside-Down Cake ... 82
Apricots ... 193, 195
Arrowroot. ... 203
Autumn ... 57

B

Baking Powder ... 199
Balmoral Almond Cake ... 117
Banana ... 195
Banana Almond Loaf ... 4
Banana and Carrot Bread (Vegan) ... 11
Banana and Passion Fruit Cake ... 8
Banana and Walnut Cake ... 3
Banana Cakes ... 1
Banana Chips ... 193
Banana Cinnamon Cake ... 9
Banana Lemon Cake ... 2
Banana Peanut Loaf ... 5
Banana Sour Cream Cake ... 6
Banana Teabread ... 5
Banana, Nut and Orange Cake (Vegan) ... 13
Beetroot and Carob Cake ... 189
Bhagavad Gita ... viii, xii, 50
Bicarbonate of Soda. ... 199
Black Treacle ... 201
Blackcurrant Tea Bread ... 69
Blueberries ... 196
Blueberry Loaf ... 75
Boiled Apricot Fruit Cake ... 124
Boiled Fruit Cake (Vegan) ... 128
Brown Sugar ... 201
Butter ... 194
Buttermilk Fruit Loaf ... 98
Buttermilk Spice Cake ... 151
Buttermilk. ... 197

C

Cakes made with vegetables ... 172
Californian Orange Cake ... 40
Candied or Glacé Fruit ... 193
Candied Peels ... 193
Caramel Banana Cake ... 14
Caraway seeds ... 200
Cardamon ... 200
Caribbean Cake ... 52
Carob ... 193
Carob Almond Cake ... 25
Carob and Orange Cake ... 29
Carob Cakes ... 15
Carob Cherry Cake (Vegan) ... 21
Carob in cooking. ... 17
Carob Lime Cake ... 28
Carob Orange Sponge ... 24
Carob Peppermint Cake ... 20
Carob Ripple Cake ... 18
Carob Sponge Cake ... 22
Carob, Cheese and Walnut Cake ... 18
Carrot and Orange Cake (Vegan) ... 48
Carrot and Orange Cake. ... 174
Carrot and Parsnip Loaf ... 191
Carrot and Prune Cake ... 181
Carrot and Walnut Cake ... 178
Carrot Cake ... 180
Carrot Coffee Cake. ... 177
Carrot Tea Bread ... 192
Carrot, Raisin and Walnut Loaf (Vegan) ... 175
Carrots ... 203
Caster Sugar ... 201
Centigrade ... xvi
Cheese ... 197
Chocolate ... 15
Chocolate, an alternative ... 16
Christmas Cake (1) ... 132
Christmas Cake (2) ... 134
Cinnamon ... 200
Cinnamon Bread ... 156
Cinnamon Ginger Cake ... 142
Citrus Cakes ... 32

Citrus Sour Cream Cake 34
Cloves 200
Coconut 193
Coconut and Caramel Cake 51
Coconut and Cherry Cake 55
Coconut Cakes 50
Coconut Orange Cake 54
Coconut Pineapple Cake 56
Coffee & Walnut Ring 161
Coffee Almond Slice 170
Coffee and Pecan Cake 171
Coffee Fudge Cake 154
Conc. Fruit Juice 202
Condensed Milk 198
Confectioners Sugar 202
Coningdale Cake 91
Contents iv
Conventions used in the book xvi
Corn Flour 195
Corn Oil 194
Corn Syrup 201
Cornflour 203
Cottage Cheese 198
Cottage Cheese Banana Bread 10
Country Tea Bread 110
Courgette (Zucchini) 203
Courgette Cake (Vegan) 186
Cream 197
Cream Cheese 197
Cream Cheese Fruit Cake 136
Cream of Tartar (Tartaric Acid) 199
Cube Sugar 201
Cumberland Buttermilk Cake 166
Currants, Raisins and Sultanas 193

D

Danish Apple Cake 68
Dark Ginger Cake 146
Date and Raisin Tea Bread 109
Date and Walnut Cake (Vegan) 87
Date Loaf (Vegan) 93
Date Sugar 202
Dates 193
Decaffeinated Coffee 203
Dedication viii
Demarara Sugar 201
Devas Food Carob Cake 30
Dorset Apple Cake 63
Double Cream 197
Dried Fruit 193
Dried Fruit Cake 123
Dundee Cake 131
Dutch Apple Tea-Bread 68

E

East Coast Prune Bread 95
Easy-Mix Carrot Cake 180
Essences 194
Evaporated Milk 198
Everyday Fruit Cake 90

F

Fahrenheit xvi
Farmhouse Sultana Cake 102
Fat-Free Fig Loaf (Vegan) 92
Fats and Oils 194
Festivals 1
  Diwali 86
Fig and Apple Loaf 77
Fig, Walnut and Ginger Cake 156
Figs 193
Flours and Grains 195
Fochabers Gingerbread 164
Food for Life 172
Fresh Apple Nut Bread 60
Fresh Fruit 195
Fresh Fruit Cakes 57
Fresh Pear and Bran Cake 74
Fruit and Nut Cake 94
Fruit Juices 196

G

Gas Mark xvi
German Spice Cake 168
Gifts for Diwali 86
Ginger 200
Ginger and Carob Cake 141
Ginger and Walnut Teabread 155
Glazed Lemon Cake 37
Golden Fruit Cake 97
Golden Gingerbread 143
Golden Syrup 201
Good Baking Practice xiii
Gooseberries 196
Gooseberry Cake 72
Granulated Sugar 201
Grape Juice 197
Greek Orange Spice Cake 160
Greek Walnut Cake 116
Guernsey Buttermilk Cake 165
Gur 202

H

Hard Cheese 198
Hazelnut Cake 114
Hazelnuts 198
Honey 201, 202

I

Iced Ginger Cake (Vegan) 147
Iced Lemon Sponge Cake 46
Icing Sugar 202
India - Land of Plenty. 122
Ingredients used in this book. 193
Introduction. x

J

Jaggery 202
Jams and Preserves 197
Jewish Orange Cake. 39
Jewish Syrup Spice Cake 152

K

Kentish Coconut Cake 53
Kurdish Apple Cake 71

L

Lebanese Date Cake 127
Lemon Almond Teabread 45
Lemon and Apricot Bread 42
Lemon Gingerbread (Vegan) 148
Lemon Yoghurt Sponge Cake 49
Lemon, Lime and Orange juice 196
Lemons 196
Liberian Plantain Gingerbread 12
Light dried fruit cakes. 86
Lime Buttermilk Cake 38
Limes 196
Lincoln Buttermilk Cake 153

M

Mace 201
Making a cake for Lord Krishna xii
Malt Extract 202
Malted Fruit Loaf 100
Maple Nut Cake (Vegan) 118
Maple Sugar Granules 202
Maple Syrup 202
Measurements. xvi
Milk 198
Milk Powder 198
Milk Products 197
Mixed Fruit 193
Mixed Nuts 199
Mixed Spice 201
Moist and rich dried fruit cakes 122
Moist Date Cake 128
Molasses 202
Mollasses 202
Mrs Beeton's Almond Cake 121
Muscovado Sugar 202
Mustard Powder 201

N

Nut Cakes 111
Nuts 198

O

Old English Cherry Cake 90
One-Stage Fruit Cake 129
Orange and Sultana Cake (Vegan) 44
Orange Cherry Bread 47
Orange Cranberry Bread (Vegan) 43
Orange Sponge Cake 36
Orange Teabread 35
Oranges 196
Other Oils 194
Oven Heat xvi
Oven Temperatures xvi
Overnight Date and Walnut Loaf 136

P

Palm Sunday Fig Cake 106
Parisian Apple Gingerbread 67
Parsnips 203
Passion Fruit and Orange Cake 41
Passion Fruit Juice. 197
Passion Fruit Tea Bread 84
Passion Fruit. 196
Patterdale Pepper Cake 149
Peanut Butter Cake 120
Peanuts. 199
Pear and Apple spread 197
Pear and Cinnamon Loaf 85
Pear and Nut Cake 76
Pears. 196
Pecan Nuts. 199
Pecan Sour Cream Cake 112
Peppermint and Rosehip Tea 203
Peppermint Essence 194
Pine Kernels. 199
Pineapple Juice. 197
Pineapple Nut Bread 76
Pineapple Tea Bread 79
Pineapples 196
Pistachios 199
Plain Flour (All Purpose Flour) 195
Plum Jam 197
Plums. 196
Poppy Seed Cake 167
Poppy seeds 200
Potato Carob Cake 184
Potato Flour 195
Potato Ginger Cake 183
Potatoes 203
Powdered sugar 202
Prune and Nut Loaf 103

Prunes 194
Pumpkin 203
Pumpkin Cake. 182
Pumpkin Pecan Cake (Vegan) 190
Pumpkin Seeds 200

Q

Quick Carob Sandwich Cake 31

R

Raising agents 199
Raspberry Jam 197
Raspberry Spice Cake. 162
Rice Syrup 202
Rich Fruit Cake 125
Rich Gingerbread 144
Rosehip Teabread (Vegan) 101
Rosemary 201
Rosewater 194
Rosewater Currant Ring 99

S

Salt 200
Scandinavian Spice Cake 150
Seed Cake 159
Seeds 200
Self-Raising Flour 195
Sesame seeds 200
Shearing Cake 158
Sienna Cake (Vegan) 135
Simnel Cake 137
Single Cream 197
Skimmed or Semi-Skimmed Milk 198
Soft Fruit Loaf 104
Somerset Treacle Cake 157
Sour Cream 197
Sour Cream Carrot Cake 173
Soya Flour 195
Soya Milk 200
Spice Cakes 138
Spiced Apple Cake 61
Spices 200
Srimad Bhagavatam viii
Sugar Substitution. 202
Sugar-Free Fruit Cake 106
Sugars and Sweeteners. 201
Sultana Apple Cake 59
Sultana Special 88
Sunflower Oil 194
Swedish Carob Cake 23
Swiss Carrot Cake 176
Syrup and Spice Teabread 163

T

Tangy Citrus Cake 34
Tea and Coffee 203
Test xiii
Texan Christmas Cake. 126
The Cosmic Power of Ginger 138
The drawbacks of chocolate 15
The Sacred Waters Of Letchmore Heath. 50
Thickening Agents 203
Toasted Coconut Cake 52
Tomato and Spice Cake 188
Tomato Raisin Loaf 185
Tomatoes 203
Turkish Carob Cake 27
Turkish Yoghurt Banana Cake 7
Tuscan Persimmon Cake 78
Tutti-Frutti Cake. 108
Tyrol Cake 100

V

Vaishnava .... vi, viii, x, xii, 1, 32, 57,86
Vaishnavism .... viii, x, xii
Vanilla Essence. 194
Vegan Apple Cake 81
Vegan Celebration Cake 130
Vegan Lemon Cake 33
Vegan Pumpkin Fruitcake 179
Vegan Spice Cake. 145
Vegetable Margarine 194
Vegetable Oil 194
Vegetables 203
Volume xvii

W

Walnut and Cherry Teabread 115
Walnut and Fruit Cake 89
Walnut Buttermilk Loaf 119
Walnuts. 199
Wedding 1
Weight xvii
What Went Wrong? xiv
Wheat Flours 195
Whipping Cream 197
Wholemeal Flour 195

Y

Yasomati's Moist Ginger Cake 139
Yoghurt 198
Yoghurt and Molasses Cake 150
Yoghurt Fig Loaf 98
Yorkshire Fruit Loaf 105